THIS ANCIENT ROAD

THIS ANCIENT ROAD

LONDON TO HOLYHEAD
A JOURNEY THROUGH TIME

ANDREW HUDSON

RedDoor

Published by RedDoor
www.reddoorpublishing.com

ISBN 978-1-910453-45-2

A CIP catalogue record for this book is available from the
British Library

Cover design: Lee-May Lim

Typesetting: Tutis Innovative E-Solutions Pte. Ltd

Maps 1 and 2: Leanne Kelman
www.lwrightdesign.co.uk

Print managed by Jellyfish Solutions Ltd

To my parents

Contents

Introduction

The Holyhead Road, in its long course towards the Irish Sea, holds much of this old romance, and not a little of a newer sort. [...] But better than the cities and towns and villages along these 260 miles is the scenery, ranging from the quiet pastoral beauties of the Home Counties to the rocks and torrents, the mountains and valleys of North Wales. This road and its story are a very epitome of our island's scenery and history.

— Charles G Harper, *The Holyhead Road:*
The Mail-coach Road to Dublin (1902)

I've always enjoyed journeys and exploration, looking at my surroundings and seeing what they tell me about the area I am in.

When I was small, I used to draw up detailed plans for the car ride to the seaside for the family holiday, labelled 'Itinerary', a word I may have picked up from the plans the AA supplied to its members in the 1960s. As a student, I enjoyed driving round rural Worcestershire as part of my researches into an eighteenth-century MP for the county. When I moved to London, to a bedsitter just off Shoot-Up Hill between Kilburn and Cricklewood – it does what it says on the sign, shoots up a hill – I became intrigued by that road. As I got to know the area better, I realised that Shoot-Up Hill was part of a very long road, the A5, which ran all the way from Marble Arch to Holyhead in Anglesey, some 250 miles from the heart of London to a far corner of Wales. One day, I thought, it would be interesting to drive the full length of that road, and maybe write about it.

What I discovered was far more fascinating than I had dared hope. The A5, based largely on the Roman Watling Street, connects Britain with Ireland, Druids with long-distance lorry drivers, ancient boroughs with New Towns, pilgrims with peddlers, holidaymakers with government officials. The route through southern England was one of the earliest metalled roads built by the Romans, and the route through Wales is one of the greatest achievements of the multi-talented Scottish engineer Thomas Telford. It has carried generals and royalty, St Alban and Disraeli, Sir John Falstaff and Samuel Pickwick – plus millions of (so-called) ordinary people making journeys for business and pleasure, on daily errands and life-changing journeys, in faith and despair, to prayer and to battle.

The A5 is one of a number of routes from London to Holyhead, and I found that these had far more touchpoints with my own past than I had realised. For much of its history, the main route didn't follow Watling Street through the Midlands, but cut a corner off, running through Coventry, Birmingham and Wolverhampton to rejoin near modern-day Telford. In the process, it went across the Stonebridge roundabout, the first landmark on most of our journeys to the seaside, along the Coventry Road into Birmingham, past where my uncle worked, and through Digbeth, where my dad's operatic society rehearsed Gilbert and Sullivan shows in a room above a pub. Some of the variants even went through Castle Bromwich, where we lived when I was small. At the London end, our holiday route followed the eighteenth-century coaches down the Holloway Road: I can still remember looking for 'A1 City signs', as the AA route put it – sadly now all gone – as we made our way to Blackfriars Bridge en route for the Kent coast.

Travelling along a road also provides an insight into the area it passes through, and what shaped it. Roads are the oldest and most basic form of transport, and the most adaptable. Almost every journey begins and ends with a trip along a road. Walking is the most basic form of transport. And the other ways of getting along a road – riding a horse or driving a cart (the options for much of the past 2000 years), cycling, taking a bus, or travelling by car – are simpler and more independent than a journey by train or plane. It's surprising that roads aren't studied more.

Paths, and then roads, were the first routes the human race actively carved out. And although some people have always travelled more than others, everyone uses the same road. In the earliest days, slaves on foot would have shared the road with the wealthy in carriages and on horseback. Today, the billionaire in the limousine drives past the youngster nursing an old banger through its last few miles – they may only meet at the service station, but they share the same stretch of tarmac.

Roads *connect* places and the people who live in them: that's their purpose. The earliest tracks linked summer and winter grazing sites for animals. The Romans built roads to consolidate their conquest of the country. Medieval roads developed to take people to market, and pilgrims to a favoured shrine. These days, we instinctively think of visiting family, taking children to school, heading to work, going to the shops, or just going for a walk or a drive. The roads adapt to facilitate these connections.

Roads also *divide*. Like rivers, they are often used as formal boundaries between counties or districts. More generally, the bigger and more important the road, the more likely that its physical presence will make it harder for people on either side to get to know each other, or to cross it to work or socialise in another area. The barrier can be psychological as well as physical.

Roads can be an *enabler* of change, which some will welcome and others not: a new bypass will mean peace and quiet for some, but economic ruin for others; a new roundabout will boost trade in one area but mean less elsewhere. In the end, however, the development of roads and the landscape along them will *reflect* wider developments in society. If an area is growing, perhaps because coal has been found there, a road will be built or improved – history suggests that it takes time for the authorities to get round to this, and nobody is keen on paying, but it happens. Similarly, roads to areas in decline will become rutted and potholed. And the buildings lining the roadside can adapt much more quickly to changes in society – old shops go out of business and new ones spring up, traditional pubs reopen as Chinese restaurants, Victorian factories become retail parks.

The London to Holyhead road provides a unique opportunity to explore these ideas. It is one of our oldest roads, one of the first built by the Romans, and the one most closely followed by a modern road – in this case the A5. It runs from the heart of London to the north-west corner of Wales, through cosmopolitan inner-city areas and suburbia, through Roman towns, market towns, and post-War New Towns, through ex-mining country, farmland and a National Park.

The seventeenth-century poet, Michael Drayton, writes about Watling Street in his poem 'Poly-Olbion'. It's a long piece, part history, part fantasy, using different ways of describing the England of the day. He gives a voice to Watling Street itself, and another character in the drama clamours for more:

> Right Noble Street, quoth he, thou hast liv'd long, gone far,
> Much traffic had in peace, much travailed in war;
> [...]
> On with thy former speech: I pray thee somewhat say.
> For, *Watling*, as thou art a military Way,
> The story of old Streets likes me wondrous well,
> That of the ancient folk I fain would hear thee tell.

Let us explore the story of this most noble of streets, the journeys along it, and the mirror it holds up to society, from London to Holyhead, from the Romans to today, through Britain and through time.

Chapter 1

Which Way?
The Roads from London to Holyhead

Afoot and light-hearted I take to the open road,
Healthy, free, the world before me,
The long brown path before me leading wherever I choose.
— 'Song of the Open Road', Walt Whitman

This book is about the London to Holyhead road, and the journeys that took place along it, and which still do. But exactly which road? The two places are about 250 miles apart, and people have been travelling that way for 2000 years or more, so it's not surprising that different routes have emerged. The A5 was codified as such by the newly established Ministry of Transport in 1923, along with other major roads. For over half its length, it follows the Roman road, which became known as Watling Street, and for rather more than that it follows the road which travellers between London and Holyhead took from medieval times through the coaching era. But the modern A5 is not exactly the same as either of these historic roads.

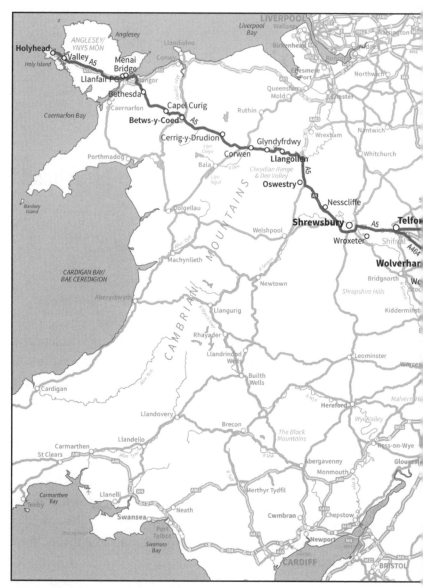

Map 1 Overview

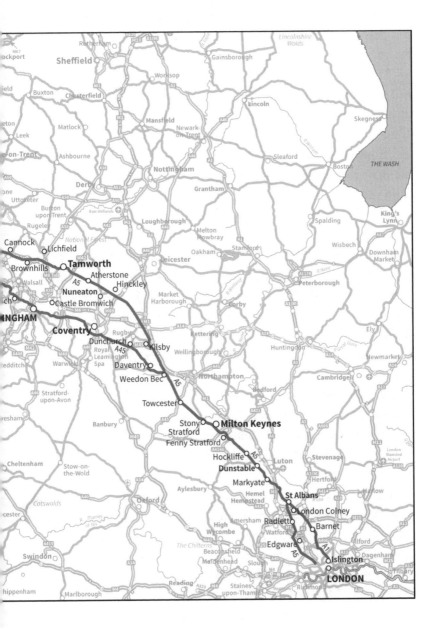

The book covers all of these routes – the way they have evolved and developed is part of the story itself. This section goes through the geography.

I've started at the London end. People from Holyhead will tell you that the Holyhead Road starts in Holyhead. As if to underline that, the first milestone on the road, installed by Thomas Telford as part of his rebuilding, shows the mileage to and from Holyhead rather than London. But my own interest in the subject arose from living near the A5 in London, so let's start from there.

The A5 today begins at Marble Arch in Central London. It was the junction of the Roman roads heading north and east from London, and it's still a major road junction today: as well as the A5, the shopping mecca of Oxford St heads east, the A40 goes west towards Notting Hill, and ultimately to Wales, and Park Lane, with its expensive hotels, points south. The Marble Arch itself was first built to stand in front of Buckingham Palace, in 1827, and was then moved to its present location in 1851.

For six centuries, from about 1200 to 1800, the area was famous for a very different reason, as the site of the Tyburn tree, where London's convicted felons met their end – there remains a plaque on the traffic island, saying, simply, 'The Site of the Tyburn Tree'.

Although a monumental structure at a major junction, in truth, Marble Arch does not feel like a grand setting-off point for one of the nation's great highways. The Arch itself is in the middle of a huge traffic island, and the surroundings are everyday rather than historic or architecturally inspiring: an Odeon cinema, Pret A Manger, and McDonald's.

The road is named Edgware Road as it begins its journey north. The eighteenth-century writer, Daniel Defoe, comments:

Figure 1 Plaque showing the location of the Tyburn tree at Marble Arch

> From Hide Park Corner [sic], just where Tyburn stands, the road
> makes one straight line without any turning, even to the very town
> of St Albans.[1]

The first mile or so combines two themes that will recur in the story:
the pencil-straight design of the Romans, and the cosmopolitan
nature of parts of urban Britain. As the road heads into Kilburn,
a ten-storey block of flats named Tollgate House provides the
first echo of the eighteenth century, when much of the road was
managed by turnpike trusts. A couple of miles further north comes
the first mention of the familiar name of Watling Street, not for
the road itself here but a small estate.

About ten miles from Marble Arch, you finally leave the
London conurbation, with the start of the Green Belt and a more

---

[1] Defoe, letter 6 (1724–26).

open stretch of country, through Radlett to St Albans. The A5 disappears for a few miles here, for the only time, and this stretch of road is now the A5183, downgraded in the late 1970s, apparently to deter heavy traffic from going through the centre of St Albans.[2]

For much of the life of the road, most travellers have taken a slightly different route from London to St Albans, through Islington and Holloway and then Barnet. This was a more direct route for travellers starting from the City of London, as opposed to Westminster.

At St Albans, the routes unite on the course carved out by the Romans as the A5 heads through Markyate to Dunstable. In the New Town of Milton Keynes, the modern A5 runs slightly east of the old Watling Street, before joining up at Stony Stratford.

From there, the road runs ramrod straight to the Roman town of Towcester, passing the racecourse on the way, and on to the small town of Weedon Bec, where the most important divide takes place. The A5 follows the Roman Watling Street north towards the Leicestershire border before turning towards the west, while the medieval route begins its journey west here, running through Daventry on the way to Coventry and the heart of the West Midlands. This was the most popular route through the coaching era, and the one improved by Thomas Telford in the early nineteenth century.

As the more direct route became established, the old Roman road fell into disuse, and the antiquarian William Stukeley, writing in the 1720s, commented:

> Here about the road is overgrown with grass and trefoil, being well nigh neglected for badness, and the trade wholly turned another way, by Coventry for that reason[3]

[2] www.sabre-roads.org.uk: The website of the Society for All British and Irish Road Enthusiasts (SABRE).

[3] William Stukeley, *Itinerarium curiosum*, quoted in Roucoux, 1984.

Things did not change for nearly two centuries, until the advent of the motor car revived the old road.

Having got to High Cross, the Roman road then takes a pretty direct course to the ford over the River Severn near Wroxeter, which was already a centre for the Cornovii tribe.

The modern A5 basically follows the Romans, through north Warwickshire, and then into Staffordshire near Tamworth and Lichfield, both just to the north of the road.

The landscape changes, reflecting the interplay of old and new industries. The road name Watling Street is much in use here, and the Roman heritage evidently continues to appeal to marketing folk: one of the modern business parks at the M42 junction near Tamworth is named Centurion Park.

The area around Brownhills and Cannock was mining country, less well known than Yorkshire or Nottinghamshire, but a dominant industry for a century or more, and still heavily built up. Past Cannock, the surroundings become rural again, with long straight stretches through Staffordshire into Shropshire and the meeting of the ways.

The alternative route, from the parting of the ways at Weedon Bec, followed roughly the course of the modern A45 through Daventry, and into the heart of the industrial West Midlands to Coventry and Birmingham, and then through Wolverhampton and on to Shifnal, mostly on the modern A41. Here, the name Holyhead Road is used at least three times, between Coventry and Allesley, on its way out of Birmingham, and again between Wednesbury and Bilston.

The route into Birmingham today is a major dual carriageway from the M42 onwards. Charles Harper, writing in 1902, mentions a small place called Elmdon. Growing up near there in the 1960s, we used occasionally to visit 'Elmdon Airport' to look at the small number of planes coming and going; these days, it is Birmingham International Airport, and you can fly to Dubai, Delhi, and even Kazakhstan.

The routes meet in what's now the Telford area, and the modern A5 to the west is the fastest stretch of the entire road, with a dual carriageway to Shrewsbury continuing from the M54. The old road could scarcely be more of a contrast: it follows a picturesque course through the countryside, eventually on a single-track road with grass growing up the middle, to the Roman town of Viroconium, today's Wroxeter.

Although the general direction of the road was east–west, the Roman road out of Viroconium runs north–south, to head for a ford over the River Severn. The old Roman road is still a footpath, heading south-east for a mile from the river to join the road from Much Wenlock to Shrewsbury.

Travellers were able to take a more direct route to Shrewsbury from the early thirteenth century when the Abbot of Lilleshall built a bridge over the Severn at Atcham, and this remained the route until the early 1990s, when the dual carriageway from the M54 was built. Strictly speaking, neither the Roman route nor the modern A5 goes through the centre of Shrewsbury itself, which was built in the middle of a meander in the Severn, so that going through it on the way to Wales would involve crossing the river twice.

From Shrewsbury, the road heads through an attractive part of rural Shropshire to the market town of Oswestry and the Welsh border. It's less clear how the Romans travelled to Holyhead through Wales, but the chances are that most travellers stayed near the coast rather than take the more direct but mountainous course of the modern road through Llangollen and Corwen, and then across sheep-farming country to cross the River Conwy at Betws-y-Coed. The quality of this stretch of the road is above all down to Thomas Telford's historic work in the early nineteenth century, justly commemorated with brown signs along the way.

An even more scenic stretch follows, alongside the River Llugwy, now in the Snowdonia National Park, passing through the walking and climbing centre of Capel Curig, to the summit of the road, at just over 1,000 feet, near the Llyn Ogwen lake. The mountain rescue post at Pen-y-benglog marks the point where the road starts to descend steeply. Snowdon itself is four to five miles to the south, the far side of the Llanberis Pass.

Figure 2 View from near the summit of the road, near the mountain rescue post at Pen-y-benglog, Snowdonia

The scenery changes again as the road heads through the slate town of Bethesda via Bangor. Near there is the Menai Suspension Bridge – another of Telford's achievements – which takes the road across the water to Anglesey. Friends who drove regularly to Holyhead, to take the boat to Dublin, said that once they got on to Anglesey, they felt they were 'nearly there'!

The route across the island is rural, passing through a series of hamlets for most of the twenty or so miles to Holyhead. Just short of there is the village of Valley, known particularly for the RAF base where Prince William was stationed and which he clearly enjoyed, commenting when he left in 2013:

This island has been our first home together, and will always be an immensely special place for us both, [...] I'm so glad to have lived on Anglesey – the mother of Wales.[4]

Holyhead is a port town. The inner harbour and admiralty pier were completed in 1821, followed by a triumphal arch marking the end of the road. There is a lot of port traffic and activity. In the middle of all the bustle stands an obelisk commemorating Captain John MacGregor Skinner, commander of the Holyhead Mail packet-ship service, who died in 1832 in a storm. Using the port is not always easy even these days – as we looked over it from near the church, we met a local lady who said that in choppy conditions, it could take an hour or more to get the alignment right for mooring.

These days, unless you are using the port, you can't get to the arch. At the end of the footpath there is an iron gate, with a letter posted on it, with a Stena letterhead, dated 29 October 2001, soon after the 9/11 atrocities in New York:

To whom it may concern,
Due to the high level of security demanded by the present world situation, this footpath will be closed for the foreseeable future.

Signed
V R Church (Captain), Harbourmaster

Understandable as this may be, it meant that, for a few years, the end of the great Holyhead road, for the visitor, was a dead-end footpath, with weeds, dead grass and cigarette ends. Thankfully, in 2007, to mark the 250th anniversary of the birth of Thomas Telford, the Institute of Civil Engineers erected a more fitting

---

[4] www.bbc.co.uk/news/uk-wales-north-west-wales-23687996 (September 2013).

14

Figure 3 The memorial stone to Thomas Telford, Holyhead

mark to the man who made a bigger contribution to the history of the road than any other single individual.

His work, however, built, often literally, on foundations laid centuries earlier by thousands of men from Mediterranean lands.

Chapter 2

Conquest and Settlement:
The Roman Road, 43–410 CE

The road they fashioned pays homage yet
To a splendour that long lies still:
And we that follow may not forget
The Roman courage, the Roman will:
And dreamers hear when the shadows fall
The stirring sound of their bugle-call;
Men from Africa, men from Gaul
Marching over the Hill!

— 'Roman Road', A G Prys-Jones[1]

The fort on the Wrekin is on top of a hill, giving a view of the surrounding area for miles around. The Iron Age men who built it did not choose it, however, for the beauty of the views over Shropshire and Wales. It was a defensive position, and they wanted to see who was coming. Standing there, looking out in the early summer haze, seeing the traffic on the different roads, you wonder if there was a moment when a native Briton, going about his daily business, suddenly heard – in the words of Prys-Jones's poem – 'The

[1] Quoted in Livingston, 1995.

stirring sound of their bugle-call', as the Romans arrived for the first time. Their road passes a mile or so to the north of the fort.

Figure 4 The Wrekin

The original purpose of the road was straightforward: conquest and domination. The Romans needed to establish their authority over the country, to take possession of it and be able to move around to key places. The thing we all learned in school – that Roman roads are straight – is a bit of an oversimplification, but the map tells its own story. They needed to get from A to B, and whenever they could, did so in a straight line. It's impressive even now to travel along, say, the stretches from Little Brickhill to Stony Stratford, or further north from Gailey to near Telford, and to see the road open out in front of you for miles. It must have been a very powerful statement to the native English who saw it happening in their midst.

There is no mystery as to why the Romans built their roads straight: it is the shortest distance, and was the easiest to survey given the techniques they developed. The road begins with a classic straight stretch heading north from Marble Arch. The route was a forest track before the Romans arrived, positioned on the slightly higher ground between the Tyburn and Westbourne streams.[2]

The Romans took the job of road-building seriously. Parts of this London stretch came to light some years ago when new pipes were being laid. The author of the classic work on Roman roads, Ivan D. Margary, says that the technique employed, with a foot of 'rammed gravel' underneath a foot of 'carefully laid nodular flints' was 'Roman construction at its best'.[3] I doubt the modern pipes will last so long.

The same basic approach was used to build most if not all the Roman roads: dig two side ditches either side of the carriageway, to create drainage; use that spoil, and other material as necessary, to build up the banking 'for the road itself, known as the "agger"; and often construct a base layer of larger stones and then a top level of fine gravel to make a smooth surface. Local materials were used whenever possible. Roads were up to thirty feet wide for major routes, though some of the stretches of Watling Street that can be traced were narrower – only eighteen feet in the Brockley Hill area, just north of London. The work would have been strenuous for the soldiers forging the route into the new country, though it must have been satisfying to see the road develop. They could not possibly have imagined that the course they set would be the basis for our journeys some 2000 years later.

You can walk in the footsteps of the Romans, and conjure up the Britain they inhabited and shaped. The ruins still standing in Verulamium (modern St Albans) frame the road. Standing beside the foundations of the London Gate, you can look back along the line of the Roman road from London, and then follow the route into the ruined town, with the River Ver on your right, and the forum and theatre on your left.

[2] Westminster, 2006.
[3] Margary, 1973.

Figure 5 Verulamium: road looking south

Figure 6 Verulamium, the old gate (1)

Figure 7 Verulamium, the old gate (2)

Further up the road to the north, there is a spot where you can explore the difference between the original course of the Roman road and the modern A5. Between Pattishall and

Figure 8 Course of the old road across fields near Pattishall

Weedon Bec, a footpath just to the east of the A5 leads into fields where you can walk along the line of the Roman road. It follows a straight but undulating course, whereas the modern road swings west to stay more on the level. Striding across the field, it's easy to imagine the passage of Roman troops, as they used the newly built road to take control of section after section of the country.

A few miles further on, there is an even clearer stretch. Just after passing through the Watford Gap, the A5 makes a bow to the east, towards the village of Kilsby and on towards the logistics hub of the Daventry International Rail Freight Terminal (DIRFT). The Roman route, however, ploughed straight on, over hillier ground, and survives as a footpath. There's a stretch where the structure characteristic of Roman roads is still very visible: the raised 'agger', with drainage ditches either side. It really is a scene mixing the old and the new: the path carries on proudly, between large warehouses belonging to Tesco and Mothercare.

The road we now know as the Roman Watling Street (actually a Saxon name, as we shall see) is not the most direct route from London to its end-point in Wroxeter in Shropshire – that would be more like the coaching route through Coventry and Birmingham. We don't know for certain why the Romans chose particular routes. Partly it may have been to connect up local tribal centres, or areas where they had already established forts. The road was built in stages, and by continuing north at Weedon Bec, they were able to branch off both east and west. There were no significant settlements at Coventry or Birmingham to attract the Romans, unlike St Albans, which was an important base for the Celtic Catuvellauni tribe.

Some pointers might also be gained from the geography. The Romans' chosen route went through the Watford Gap, the pass between hills which gave its name to the service station on the M1. The Roman road was the first major communications channel to use it, joined centuries later by the Leicester Line of the Grand Union Canal, then by the railway from London to Birmingham (now the West Coast Main Line), and finally by the M1 in 1959. All four still run within a quarter of a mile of each other through the Gap.

From there, the Roman road went on to Tripontium, a fort just in modern-day Warwickshire, where it was possible to cross the Avon, on the way to Venonis (today's High Cross). There was a settlement in the area even before Roman times, and Venonis became the junction of Watling Street with the Fosse Way, which linked Exeter and Lincoln. The signpost today does refer to the Fosse Way (though not to Watling Street), but there are very few buildings, and it takes an effort of the imagination to see it as the strategically important junction it once was.

Figure 9 Course of the old road near Kilsby

To be confident of establishing the control they sought, there was a clear case for the Romans to go to Anglesey (then known as Mona): the island was a point of vulnerability. That argument certainly appealed to Suetonius Paulinus, who took over as governor of the embryonic province of Britain in 58 CE. The Roman historian, Tacitus, characterises him as a competitive type, who wanted to show his seniors in Rome that he was the equal of other generals who were breaking new ground in other parts of the empire. So, according to Tacitus, 'Suetonius planned to attack the island of Mona, which although thickly populated had also given sanctuary to many refugees'.[4]

By the year 61, Suetonius's army would have been able to pass through a number of established forts on the way north. Excavations in Verulamium suggest that work began on the road there in the first few years after the Romans arrived in 43 CE.[5] The Catevellauni there were not as opposed to Roman rule as many tribes, and may even have welcomed it – they had already been trading with the Roman Empire – and any resistance in the Verulamium area had collapsed within a few months. Other areas, by contrast, fought hard.

Between there and London, evidence suggests that the Brockley Hill site was occupied from about the year 50 CE. Heading north, there were eleven known Roman settlements by 61, from Dunstable (Durocobrivis) to Wroxeter (Viroconium).

Once in Wales, Suetonius will have had a harder journey, probably relying on local tracks rather than Roman-built roads. When he reached the Menai Straits, which stood between him and Anglesey, flat-bottomed boats took the infantry across, while

---

[4] Tacitus, Book XIV (trans. Grant, 1956). All extracts reproduced by permission of Penguin Books Ltd.
[5] This section draws on Roucoux (1984) and website: h2g2 Watling Street – A Journey through Roman Britain.

the cavalry forded and swam. He was greeted by a dramatic sight, at least according to Tacitus:

> The enemy lined the shore in a dense armed mass. Among them were black-robed women with dishevelled hair like Furies ... Close by stood Druids, raising their hands to heaven and screaming dreadful curses.[6]

The Romans won the battle, and Suetonius put an end to some local customs, including that of consulting the gods 'by means of human entrails'.[7]

Suetonius then heard of a rebellion. Boudicca, widow of Prasutagus, King of the Iceni, had been flogged by Roman soldiers, and their daughters raped. The Iceni rebelled, joined by the Trinobantes and others, and created havoc. In the words of Tacitus:

> The natives enjoyed plundering [...] They could not wait to cut throats, hang, burn and crucify [...] 70,000 Roman and provincial deaths are estimated.[8]

Suetonius clearly had to get back to the south-east quickly, demonstrating the need for a good road. One modern writer on Tacitus says that he would have 'come straight down what is now the A5',[9] but the journey was not quite that simple: the A5 route across Snowdonia was not established at the time, and it seems likely that the road from Wroxeter via Chester and St Asaph to Holyhead was only finished after Agricola completed the conquest of North Wales, about 77–78.[10]

When he did reach the south-east, Suetonius decided to sacrifice London 'to save the province as a whole'. Inhabitants

---

[6] Tacitus (trans. Grant, 1956).
[7] Ibid.
[8] Ibid.
[9] Miller, 1987.
[10] Margary, 1973.

who could not leave with him 'were slaughtered by the enemy. Verulamium suffered the same fate'.[11]

He then manoeuvred to find an advantageous time and place for the battle with Boudicca. We don't know with any certainty where the combat took place: some evidence points to an area near Mancetter in Warwickshire, though the town museum in Towcester makes a case for it being in their local area.[12]

Suetonius massed a force of about 10 000 men. Boudicca drove round in a chariot to rally her troops:

> Old people are killed, virgins raped. But the gods will grant us the vengeance we deserve.[13]

Sadly for her, the invocation to the gods did not prevail against the Romans' combination of foot-soldiers, cavalry, and volleys of javelins. Almost 80 000 Britons fell, and Boudicca poisoned herself. In spite of his victory, however, Suetonius did not get the career advancement he sought: according to Tacitus, internal rivalries in Rome meant that he was 'superseded for not terminating the war'.[14]

There were, nonetheless, no further battles as dramatic as those of Suetonius, as the Romans established the full network of towns and forts they needed to consolidate their hold over Britain. The surviving evidence along Watling Street gives some interesting insights.

Verulamium became one of the largest towns in Roman Britain. The Basilica combined the functions of town hall, religious centre and law court, while the Forum was the commercial hub. Watling Street was at the heart of much of this: there is evidence, for instance, of a carpenter's workshop looking out directly on to

[11] Tacitus (trans. Grant, 1956).
[12] Graham Webster, 'Boudicca', referred to in the website: British History Online.
[13] Tacitus (trans. Grant, 1956).
[14] Ibid.

the road. The Roman temple stood where the road divided the town – it now sits in the middle of football pitches in modern-day Verulamium Park in St Albans. A well-preserved hypocaust (heating system) and mosaic floor testify to the wealth and importance of many who lived in the town.

The existence of these facilities shows that, once they had established their domination over the country, the Romans used the road for a range of political and economic purposes. Certainly, soldiers would still have been on the march, either individually, or in groups as one legion took over from another at an important garrison. But increasingly, the road would be taken up by men on horseback, or using two-wheeled carts pulled by mules or ponies, to move goods around. Wine from the Continent was driven to the homes of the wealthy in places like Verulamium, paid for perhaps by the export of hides. Rich and poor alike used pottery vessels for cooking and storage, and the work of a number of different potters who we know by name has been found in locations up and down the road. Products by Albinus have been found in Verulamium and nearby Bricket Wood, as well as in Colchester; Matugenus's work was found in Brockley Hill, in north London, as well as Verulamium; and Marinus's products appear in Mancetter in Warwickshire, as well as Radlett (near Verulamium) and Colchester.

As the Roman system of governance became more structured, new classes of traveller emerged. High-ranking officials, military and civilian, visited different parts of the country to pass on decrees or advice, and no doubt to report back on what they found. One of the places they stayed was Wall (Roman Letocetum), in Staffordshire, where the surviving remains show a town geared up for visitors concerned with the administration of Roman Britain. Wall was a staging post, set up to provide both hospitality and vehicles for these high-ranking officials, who were accommodated in some comfort in 'mansiones' in the town, where they could eat, take advantage of the baths, and change their horses before pressing on. Less-welcome visitors were the government agents known first as 'frumentarii' and then 'agentes in rebus'. Their original role was to assist the movement of forces, but in practice they were government spies. More senior military staff may have taken overall charge of the stretch of road up to Wroxeter.[15] Some of the soldiers based in Letocetum, known as 'stationarii', may have had a role in corralling local people into mending the road when necessary.

Wroxeter itself shows how a settlement built originally to establish control became a major centre for residence and trade – it was the fourth largest town in Roman Britain. It was built as a fort in the 50s CE, by soldiers of the fourteenth legion, who were replaced by the twentieth in the 60s. By around the year 90, the garrison was relocated to Chester, but rather than disappearing, Wroxeter developed as a major civilian town.[16] It owed its prosperity in part to its location connecting up a number of routes: north to Whitchurch, west to Forden Gaer in mid-Wales, and south to Leintwardine and Monmouth.[17]

Walking around the ruins at Wroxeter, the importance of the town becomes obvious, reflecting the civilisation that had been developed over the Roman centuries. The ruined basilica still towers above head height, the remains of a really imposing building. The shops were neatly arranged along the streets in the town itself, and the size and quality of these premises indicate these were for relatively prosperous customers, whose own houses were bigger still, arranged to enjoy a clear view over the Shropshire countryside. Livestock would have been brought along the local roads and tracks to market in Wroxeter, but the excavations suggest that the cattle market was placed on relatively high ground, so that the smells quickly blew away.

[15] Gould, 1998.
[16] Higgins, 2013.
[17] Hooke, 2006.

Figure 10 Wroxeter ruins

Wroxeter also offers a glimpse into the world-view of some Roman soldiers who came there in the course of their duties. A tombstone includes the inscription:

> Titus Flaminius [...] from Faventia, aged 45, of 22 years service, a soldier of the 14th legion Gemina; I did my service and now am here. Read this and be either more or less fortunate in your lifetime. The gods prohibit you from the wine, grape, and water when you enter Tartarus. Live honourably while your star grants you time for life.[18]

For a long time, historians assumed that the Roman site was abandoned as soon as the successors of Titus Flaminius left in the early fifth century, though recent research suggests that the town

---

[18] Shrewsbury Museum.

was occupied into the sixth or seventh century.[19] But its importance waned in time, and Wroxeter became the small village it is today. It did, however, attract attention again in the mid-nineteenth century: in February 1859 workmen began excavating the baths complex, and within weeks, visitors had flocked to the area, with Charles Dickens among them. The landowner made the site available for public viewing, so Wroxeter became one of the first archaeological visitor attractions in the country. It's well presented now by English Heritage: given its history and accessibility, it deserves more attention than it gets.

The ruins did inspire A E Housman, who drew on the fate of Wroxeter, or Uricon as he calls it, to write about the impermanence of life in his poem 'On Wenlock Edge'. He imagines a Roman watching the wind blow, and concludes:

> The gale, it plies the saplings double,
> It blows so hard, 'twill soon be gone:
> Today the Roman and his trouble
> Are ashes under Uricon.

The decline of Uricon was only one of many changes in the history of the road as the Romans withdrew.

---

[19] See White and Barker, 1998, and the English Heritage website on Wroxeter Roman City.

Chapter 3

Waetlingastraet: Saints and Boundaries: From the Romans to Domesday

The frontier ran up the River Lygean to its source, then straight to Bedanford and up the River Usan, to Waetlingastraet.
— Treaty of Alfred and Guthrum, 886[1]

The Anglo-Saxons did not build great highways in the way that the Romans did, but so far from the mythical Dark Ages, the period from the departure of the Romans in 410 CE to the Norman Conquest in 1066 saw plenty of new developments. Troops continued to march along the road, and at times across it, but in calmer times new types of journey emerged. The road also acquired the name of Watling Street, still much in evidence today.

One of the main changes actually had its origins in the later Roman era, beginning near the town of Verulamium: the growth of journeys as pilgrimages.

In his *A History of the English Church and People*, written in 731, the Venerable Bede tells the story of the martyrdom of St Alban, which took place around 301, when the Romans were not yet

---

[1] Quoted in Roucoux, 1984.

converted to Christianity. Alban gave shelter to a Christian priest who was being persecuted.[2] Impressed by this priest's devotion and his teaching, Alban himself became a Christian. When the priest's pursuers caught up with him, Alban donned the priest's cloak and substituted himself as prisoner. He stuck to his new faith in the face of threats and torture, and was condemned to death by decapitation. Even before Alban was martyred, miracles began to take place: a river opened up for him to walk across; the first executioner was so moved by this that he fell at Alban's feet; and when Alban asked God to provide water, a spring bubbled up. Finally, when Alban was put to death, the replacement executioner's eyes dropped out.

Bede concludes:

> Saint Alban suffered on the twenty-second day of June near the city of Verulamium, which the English now call Verlamacaestir or Vaeclingacaestir. Here, when the peace of Christian times was restored, a beautiful church worthy of his martyrdom was built, where sick folk are healed and frequent miracles take place to this day.[3]

The pull of St Albans was given a boost a century after Alban's death, as a by-product of a visit from Germanus, the Bishop of Auxerre, to France. As well as taking part in theological debates, Germanus cured a ten-year-old girl of blindness by touching her eyes with holy relics. His work complete, Bede reports that he 'paid a visit to the tomb of the blessed martyr Alban to return thanks to God through him'. Germanus had Alban's tomb opened up, and deposited fresh relics of saints in it.

> And when he had reverently deposited these relics, Germanus took away with him a portion of the earth from the place where

---

[2] Bede (trans. Sherley-Price, 1968).
[3] Bede, Book 1, Chapter 7.

the blessed martyr's blood had been shed. This earth was seen to have retained the martyr's blood, which had reddened the shrine where his persecutor had grown pale with fear. As a result of these events, a great number of people were converted to our Lord on the same day.[4]

Two and a half centuries later, another pilgrimage site began to emerge nearly 100 miles further along the road at Lichfield. Around 667, a monk named Chad became Bishop of the Mercians and the people of Lindsey, based at Lichfield. Bede records that he 'administered the diocese in great holiness of life after the example of the early Fathers'.[5] After his death in 672, miracles of healing began to take place near where he was buried. Bede gives one particular example:

> A madman wandering at large arrived there one evening, and passed the night in church unnoticed and unheeded by the watchman. And in the morning, to the amazement and delight of all, he left the place in his right mind.[6]

The city became a place of pilgrimage from about 700, when the first cathedral was dedicated.[7] Chad's tomb, according to Bede, gave a particular opportunity to pilgrims:

> Chad's burial place is covered by a wooden tomb made in the form of a little house with an aperture in the wall, through which those who visit it out of devotion may insert their hand and take out some of the dust. They mix this in water and give it to sick men or beasts to drink, by which means their ailment is quickly relieved and they are restored to the longed for joys of health.[8]

[4] Ibid, Book 1, Chapter 18.
[5] Ibid, Book 4, Chapter 3.
[6] Ibid, Book 4, Chapter 3.
[7] Lichfield Cathedral website.
[8] Bede, Book 4, Chapter 3.

This unusual tomb was replaced some time in the eighth century with a chest that featured a carved angel, produced in Mercia for Lichfield, which is evidence of the wealth and skills available at the time. It was probably damaged and then buried as a result of later Viking raids, and only came to light again in 2003.

Pilgrimage thus became one of the main purposes for journeys along the road in Saxon times, and it was to become more important yet in the medieval period.

Lichfield became more prominent in the reign of Offa, King of Mercia from 757 to 796, who attempted to make it the religious centre of this part of England. He persuaded the Pope to establish a new archbishopric there in 787. It is not entirely clear why, but the country at the time was split between several small kingdoms, and Offa was probably trying to build up his power-base to counter rivals in the south of England. The new archbishop had authority over a large swathe of the middle of the country from

Figure 11 Lichfield Cathedral, the Angel carving on an eighth-century chest

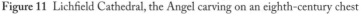

Herefordshire to the east coast, though the arrangement did not last long after Offa's death.

Christianity gradually made its mark on the physical landscape through the Anglo-Saxon period. As well as the main centres at St Albans, Lichfield and Shrewsbury, churches were built in a number of smaller places. Although Wroxeter lost its importance as a town, its church has some carved stone panels of animals which may date from the late eighth or early ninth centuries.[9] The church a few miles away at Atcham is the only one in England dedicated to St Eata, a seventh-century bishop: it dates back to before 1075, when the chronicler Orderic Vitalis was baptised there. It is not certain whether any of the original building survives, though some of the carvings incorporated into the walls may well be from that era.

If Lichfield was the spiritual hub of the Midlands, the nearby town of Tamworth was more important politically and economically. As well as being near the Roman road, it had the advantage of being at the meeting point of two rivers, the Anker and the Tame. In the time of Offa, Tamworth was the capital of Mercia.

Evidence of the importance of this area emerged in a particularly spectacular fashion on 5 July 2009. A metal detector enthusiast named Terry Herbert was out in farmland, just south of the A5, not far from his home in Hammerwich, near Lichfield, when he made a discovery which he and his fellow enthusiasts could only dream about: the largest collection of Anglo-Saxon gold and silver ever found. The Staffordshire Hoard, as the find has become known, comprises more than 3500 items of the highest quality workmanship in gold, silver and garnets.

It is an intriguing find, one that experts will continue to study for many years to come. The work so far suggests the treasures date to the seventh or eighth centuries. However, big questions

[9] White and Barker, 1998.

Figure 12 Staffordshire Hoard: example of work

remain. The items are mainly military – parts of swords and shields and helmets – but include nothing that women would have worn, no utensils, and no ironware. And they are almost all damaged, apparently deliberately. So why was the hoard in Hammerwich? Were its owners pagans or Christians? Is it significant that it is buried near the old Roman road? Did an army march along the road, proudly sporting their gold-embellished kit, only to be defeated and despoiled? Answering these questions should tell us more not just about the hoard, but about the people it belonged to and their society.[10]

Peace in England came under attack from the Danish invasions, which began in earnest in 865. After two decades of fighting, a settlement was reached in 886, after King Alfred

[10] www.staffordshirehoard.org.uk.

occupied London, and in the process established his authority across the Anglo-Saxon kingdoms – in the words of the *Anglo-Saxon Chronicle*, 'all the English people submitted to him, except those who were in captivity to the Danes'.[11] A dividing line of sorts between those groups was established by the Treaty of Alfred and Guthrum (the Danish leader), which set the western boundary of Guthrum's kingdom as running from the Thames up the River Lea to its source near Luton, making a straight line to Bedford and then heading westwards along the River Ouse to Watling Street. In his classic work *Anglo-Saxon England*, Sir Frank Stenton adds, 'Beyond this point it is probable that Watling Street formed the western boundary of Guthrum's country'.[12] The road would not have been chosen by accident: presumably, it was already emerging in practice as the dividing line between the two sets of forces.

This Treaty was the first official document to use the name Watling Street, which is of Saxon origin – it is ironic that probably the best-known Roman road in the country should have a Saxon name. It comes from the same root as one of the newer names for the Roman Verulamium quoted by Bede, 'Uaeclingacaestir' (or Vaeclingacaestir) – the town of the Uaeclingas, a local tribe. In later manuscripts, this became Waetlingacaiestir, and the road which ran through the area became Waetlingastraet – the Old English term '*straet*' tended to be used for a Roman road.

Watling Street remains the boundary between Warwickshire and Leicestershire to this day, for some twenty miles. The original boundary also brings a legacy in the place names either side. Scandinavian names are relatively common in Leicestershire – including, for instance, '*thorpe*' meaning a settlement of secondary scale, or '*toft*' (site of a house) – but not so common south of Watling Street.[13]

---

[11] *Anglo-Saxon Chronicle*.
[12] Stenton, 1947.
[13] Cameron, 1996.

The Holyhead road played host to more of the struggles for supremacy between the English and the Danes in the tenth century. In 910, King Edward the Elder won an important battle at Tettenhall, just north of modern Wolverhampton. The following year, Edward's sister, Aethelflaed, was recognised as 'Lady of the Mercians' after the death of her husband – she was the true daughter of Alfred the Great, ruled Mercia for eight years, planned expeditions against her enemies and even led her troops in person. She played a significant part in the King's success against the Danes over the coming years. In 913, Aethelflaed fortified Tamworth, and also built fortresses at Stafford, Warwick and Bridgnorth, among other places. [14] Although these were founded with defensive considerations in mind, they also gave a boost over time to a town's trading position.

Aethelflaed died in Tamworth in 918. I had assumed that names like hers had died with the Saxon era, but discovered on a visit to Tamworth Castle that Thomas Cook (a textile manufacturer, not the travel agent), who lived in the castle in the late nineteenth century, had called his daughter Aethelflaeda. He does not, however, appear to have started a new trend.

Edward continued to establish control over areas of the country previously held by the Danes. He won battles in the Towcester area in 917, and reinforced the town's defences. [15] The following year, 'all the people of Mercia, who had been under allegiance to Aethelflaed turned in submission to him'. [16] The Saxons held sway for some time, until in 943, says the *Anglo-Saxon Chronicle*, 'Anlaf stormed Tamworth and there was great slaughter on both sides: the Danes had the victory and carried great booty away with them'.

[14] *Anglo-Saxon Chronicle.*
[15] *Anglo-Saxon Chronicle.*
[16] *Anglo-Saxon Chronicle.*

The road was again used as a boundary: the Archbishops of Canterbury and York brokered a treaty which gave the invading army, led by Anlaf, authority over the region between Watling Street and the Northumbrian border, though the English King, Edmund, was able to restore his authority within a year or two.

With the focus of the periodic fighting further to the north, the climate was more favourable to the development of trade. Historians continue to debate the relative importance of defence and trade or governance in the development of Anglo-Saxon towns.[17] The same applies to roadways, though there are examples of routes which reflect trade links. Most of the main market towns did not come to prominence until the medieval period, but St Albans, Towcester, Tamworth, Lichfield and Shrewsbury were certainly established in the Anglo-Saxon period, and there is evidence that both Shrewsbury and Tamworth minted coins. The chroniclers record the names and deeds of royalty, great warriors and saints, but the vast majority of journeys along Watling Street and other roads were short journeys to market made by local people selling their wares and buying small amounts of other goods with the proceeds.

By the end of the Anglo-Saxon period, there are indications that traffic, at least on the southern stretch of the road, was quite busy. This is partly because the growing city of London sucked in resources from the rest of the country as food, woollen goods and other things headed for the capital. The *Gesta Abbatorum* from the Abbey Church of St Albans records that Abbot Leofstan, who was in office around 1050, took action to improve the road:

> Taking pity on all those who were in peril, such as travellers and merchants and also pilgrims who came to the church of St Albans for the expiation of their sins and the well being of

---

[17] Summarised in Hooke, 1981, for example.

their bodies, [Leofstan] made the roads safer and had the dense woods from the slopes of the Chilterns as far as London cut back, especially along the royal road which is called Watling Street, smoothed out bits of difficult going, built bridges and had steep tracts of road reduced to a safe level.[18]

According to some sources, Leofstan also granted the nearby manor of Flamstead to a knight named Turnot and his companions Waldef and Thurman, on the condition that they keep Watling Street 'free from robbers and dangerous beasts'.[19]

The St Albans chronicler is, of course, not an entirely independent witness, but it is interesting that he drew attention to the needs of travellers and merchants as well as pilgrims as the beneficiaries of Leofstan's efforts. Unfortunately for road users elsewhere, Leofstan's enthusiasm for civil engineering does not appear to have been matched in other parts of the country.

The Anglo-Saxon era came to an abrupt end with the Norman Conquest in 1066. The Normans took a number of steps to establish their authority, including building castles at strategic points. Bury Mount, which still stands in Towcester, is the remains of a Norman fortification which may date back to the eleventh century, along with fortifications in West Felton in Shropshire.

William the Conqueror also took a very different step to assess his kingdom. Early in 1086, a new set of travellers spread out over the roads of England. In the words of the *Anglo-Saxon Chronicler*:

The King had important deliberations and exhaustive discussions with his council about this land, how it was peopled, and with what sort of men. Then he sent his men all over England into

[18] Quoted in Webb, 2000.
[19] Victoria County History: Hertfordshire Vol 2, 1908, at: www.british-history.ac.uk. The reference to Watling Street specifically comes from a modern notice board in Flamstead itself.

every shire to ascertain how many hundreds of 'hides' of land there were in each shire, and how much land and livestock the king himself owned in the country, and what annual dues were lawfully his from each shire. [...] So very thoroughly did he have the inquiry carried out that there was not a single "hide", not one virgate of land, [...] not even one ox, nor one cow, nor one pig, which escaped his notice in this survey.[20]

The *Chronicle* also brings out that the surveyors made records not just of the King's possessions, but those of the Church and of all other landowners. It was an epoch-making exercise, recording the basis of taxation, bringing together the resources of the new feudal order, and recording ownership where it had been disputed and settled in court. In short, it recorded the outcome of conquest. Not for nothing did the resulting work become known to the English as *Domesday*, or Book of Judgement.[21]

The commissioners dispatched by William the Conqueror took evidence on oath from the Sheriff, the barons and other local notables. Shires were grouped into 'circuits': along Watling Street, circuit III covered (among other places) Middlesex through to Buckinghamshire, and circuit IV took it from Northamptonshire to Staffordshire. Shropshire and Cheshire were in a circuit of their own.[22]

To be sure of accuracy and impartiality, these results were then checked. Robert Losinga, Bishop of Hereford, wrote in 1086:

Other investigators followed the first; and men were sent into provinces they did not know, and where they were themselves unknown, so they might be able to check the first survey.

[20] *Anglo-Saxon Chronicle* (ed. and trans. Garmonsway).
[21] Sally Harvey's *Domesday: Book of Judgement* explains the concept in detail.
[22] Harvey, 2014.

Let's imagine that, rather than work in circuits, a commissioner had worked his way up Watling Street in 1086. What would he have found?

England consisted largely of small settlements known as 'vills'.[23] Land values were higher in the south of England: one of the leading authorities on the topic, H C Darby, calculates that rural holdings were worth around 50 shillings per square mile in Middlesex, Hertfordshire, Bedfordshire and Buckinghamshire, but fell away through the Midlands, and even more in Staffordshire and Shropshire, though the areas around Lichfield and Shrewsbury did better. The poorer counties were also more thinly populated for the most part. So the north–south divide which challenges economic policymakers today is clearly not new. In 1086, it reflected, in part at least, the impact of the Conquest itself: there is plenty of evidence that before 1066 parts of the north had been prosperous and productive, but William had laid waste to it, to establish his rule.

Other evidence suggests that the commissioners would have found churches to worship in, though the *Domesday Book* doesn't record them consistently – the different circuit surveyors worked in different ways. Many villages in Northamptonshire, Leicestershire and Warwickshire, for instance, are recorded as having priests but not churches, but that may not have been the case.

Most of the main places now on the road are in *Domesday* – notable exceptions include Dunstable, still a Roman ruin, and Oswestry, mentioned only for its castle. This is not definite evidence that there wasn't a settlement there – the remit of the *Domesday* surveyors did not cover towns as such, still less roads – and the major established borough of Tamworth is not mentioned at all, along with London and Winchester, though it is not clear why.

Many people will be surprised that Milton Keynes is mentioned, under the name of Middeltone, along with many of

[23] Darby, 1977, Maitland, 1897.

the neighbouring villages that now make up the city. Telford is not, of course, mentioned by name, but many of its component parts are. In some areas, there is a pattern of settlements along the road, but in others there isn't: the key factor seems to be the availability of water, from a spring or a river, rather than ancient road links.[24] By 1086, Anglo-Saxon patterns of trade and settlement had led to the development of a pretty dense network of trackways in some places, and the Roman roads were not always the most important.[25]

Starting at the London end, there is nothing on the Roman Watling Street, but there are several mentions of Islington, on the alternative route out of the city. The very first entry will give some flavour of what is recorded:

> In Islington, the Canons of St Paul's have 2 hides. Land for 1½
> ploughs. 1 plough there; ½ possible.
> 3 villagers with 1 virgate.
> Pasture for the village livestock.
> The value of this land is and was 40s.
> It lay and lies in the lordship of St Paul's Church.[26]

The survey proceeds in this very structured way, shire by shire. There is a substantial section in the Hertfordshire volume for Land of St Albans Church. The town itself 'answers for 10 hides'. As well as the measures quoted for Islington, it records 'There are a further 12 cottagers, a park for woodland beasts, and a pond for fish'. Further on, there is an enigmatic entry for Redbourn: 'Land for 1 plough, but it is not there; only 2 smallholders'.

Some of the entries in Bedfordshire go into more detail. Houghton Regis was 'a household manor of the King's'. As well as

---

[24] Darby, 1977.

[25] Taylor, 1979.

[26] All references and quotations are from *Domesday Book* (ed. and trans. Morris, 1975). A hide is a unit of land measurement, about 120 acres. It served as a unit of tax assessment. A virgate is a fraction of a hide, usually a quarter.

the detail on hides and ploughs, there is information about taxation, giving insights into the sophistication of the arrangements William inherited, and the complexity of local circumstances:

> In total, it pays £10 a year by weight and half a [day's provisions] in wheat, honey, and other things which belong to the King's revenue; from petty customary duties and from 1 pack-horse 65s; from the customary dog dues 65s; to the Queen 2 ounces of gold; from the increase which Ivo Tallboys put on £3 by weight and 20s in white silver; 1 ounce of gold to the Sheriff.

In Bedfordshire, we also encounter the first female landowner on the journey north: 'Azelina, wife of Ralph Tallboys, holds 1½ hides in Battlesden from the King'.

There are not one but three entries for Middeltone (Milton Keynes), with different spellings. The fullest gives more information on the make-up of the population:

> Godric Cratel holds 8 ½ hides from the King as one manor in Milton. Land for 10 ploughs; in lordship 2 ½ ploughs; ½ possible. 18 villagers with 6 smallholders have 8 ploughs. 6 slaves; 1 mill at 6s 8d; meadow for 8 ploughs. In total the value is and was 100s; before 1066 £8. Queen Edith held this manor.

There is an insight into change in Towcester: among the King's holdings it records that 'The smiths paid 100s; now nothing'.

Catthorpe, now mostly known for the M1/M6 junction, is mentioned, with two ploughs and a mill. The authors in Leicestershire saw fit to record where a village had a priest, along with the number of villagers.

The Warwickshire volume has six entries recorded as Land of Countess Godiva. Legend has it that 'Lady Godiva' rode naked, covered only by her hair, through the streets of Coventry to protest against the taxes her husband, Leofric, Earl of Mercia, levied on his tenants. There is stronger evidence that she and her husband were the benefactors of several monasteries in the Midlands, and that she lived on as a widow and landowner after 1066, but had died by the time of *Domesday*. Her holdings included land in Atherstone, with three hides, and the only mention of Coventry itself in the Book, with five hides, fifty villagers and twelve smallholders. That was still much bigger than Birmingham, with five villagers and four smallholders, though other places now part of the city are recorded separately: the neighbouring entry is for Edgbaston, where my mother now lives, with three villagers and seven smallholders. This entry suggests territory that was not very fertile: the Birmingham Botanical Gardens today shows how things can change!

The Staffordshire volume has plenty of entries, not least along Watling Street, but is quite slim as they are short. The exception is an extensive entry for Lichfield: 'The church held it itself', with seventy-three ploughs, and more property 'in lordship'. The Staffordshire volume betrays the recent Danish influence, in that many entries measure land by the 'carucate', which was 'normally the equivalent of a hide, in former Danish areas'.[27]

Finally, the Shropshire volume tells the story of the fortunes of the county. There are plenty of entries in the east of the county. The established borough of Shrewsbury has plenty of detail across ten entries, spanning land owned by Earl Roger of Montgomery, one of the Conqueror's lieutenants, and various religious establishments. It also notes that the burgesses of Shrewsbury objected that they still had to pay the same amount of tax as in 1066, even though the Earl had taken over a large number of premises within the town.

As you get further west, the impact of war becomes clearer. West Felton, for instance, falls within the holding of Reginald the Sheriff under Earl Roger:

[27] Notes from the Domesday edition.

A man-at-arms holds from him. Siward held it. ½ hide. Land for 1 plough.

It was and is waste.

Whether through raids from Wales just across the border, or to make space for the King and his friends to hunt deer, tracts of West Shropshire were indeed 'waste'.

Domesday gives us a unique record of the state of the nation in the late eleventh century. It is a partial record: it doesn't mention roads, and barely talks about buildings as such. Few survive from the Anglo-Saxon era, so it is harder to imagine what the roadscape would have looked like. Fortunately many more survive from the centuries which followed.

Chapter 4

Markets, Bridges, Pilgrims, and Progresses: The Medieval Road

When in April the sweet showers fall
And pierce the drought of March to the root, and all
The veins are bathed in iquor of such power
As brings about the engendering of the flower ...
The people long to go on pilgrimages.
— Geoffrey Chaucer, *The Canterbury Tales*

The medieval period saw a growth in travel for a variety of reasons: trade was the most common; pilgrimages, long and short, became more popular; and landowners had to visit their properties – medieval monarchs were particularly active in getting around the kingdom. The infrastructure expanded to match: bridges were built, and inns sprang up in the popular destinations and staging posts. The same does not seem to have happened to the surface of the roads, where there is no evidence of developments beyond patching up the Roman roads.

Watling Street remained one of the most important routes in the country. It was accorded special status in the *Leges Edwardi Confessoris*, which in spite of its title was written in the twelfth century, even though the laws it documents may date back to Edward's reign in the mid-eleventh century.

> There are many types of the king's peace: […] another which the roads have, that is Watling Street, Fosse Way, Iknield Way, and Ermine Street, of which two extend for the length of the kingdom, the other two across the width.

This did not apply to most routes, since 'Other roads from city to cities, from boroughs to boroughs, on which people travel to markets or for their other business affairs, are under the law of the county'.[1]

These laws also confirm the role of Watling Street, 'Watlingstrate' in the Latin, as a boundary:

> Yorkshire, Lincolnshire, Nottinghamshire, Leicestershire, Northamptonshire and up to Watling Street, and the eight beyond Watling Street are under the law of the English.[2]

While Watling Street remained in use, travellers had established a new route from London to the West Midlands and Wales between the departure of the Romans and the fourteenth century. We know this from a medieval map known as the Gough Map, produced around 1360.

The Gough Map is an intriguing document – the first map we have that purports to be geographically accurate rather than symbolic – and full of interest. Roads are shown as straight lines between two towns, with distances marked in Roman numerals – these distances were reasonably well understood, so that itineraries could be prepared for Royal progresses, or justices on circuit.[3]

---

[1] *Leges Edwardi Confessoris*, ed. Bruce O'Brien, at Earlyenglishlaws.ac.uk, ch. 12. The earliest version of the Leges probably comes from early in the reign of Stephen, which began in 1135.

[2] Ibid, ch. 30. 'The eight' refers to the eight hundreds of Northamptonshire, which lay south and west of Watling Street.

[3] Parsons, 1970.

A traveller using the Gough Map would head out of London through Barnet, rather than Edgware, and then pick up the old Roman route via St Albans and Dunstable to Stony Stratford. At that point, the road divides between a route north to Doncaster, and the road north-west, via Daventry, Coventry, Coleshill, Lichfield and Stone, where there is another divide between a circuitous route to Chester via Shrewsbury, and a more direct one to Carlisle.

The new route connected up places that had grown in importance since Roman times. Dunstable and Coventry were established as boroughs, with certain privileges and obligations attached, in the twelfth century, and Birmingham, Wolverhampton and Oswestry followed in the thirteenth century. Many more places had markets: there were about five times as many markets permitted as there were full boroughs – Stony Stratford, for instance, can trace its market charter back to 1194.

Market day was clearly the big day of the week, not just for the town itself but for people from the nearby villages and hamlets. The chance to trade was much more regulated than it is today, so it was vital to get the right day – making for stability. Lichfield's market day changed from Sunday to Friday in 1308, and has remained the same ever since. The market square would be packed with local farmers and labourers trading wool and corn. Richer people would be looking for more unusual produce, such as metal wares or spices, which would not be available in smaller villages. It was also the occasion to consult a lawyer or a doctor. The roads into town in the morning would be very busy with rich and poor, buyers and sellers, along with their sheep and cattle, going about their business.

Dunstable is an example of how the reason for the emergence of a borough could be both political and economic. It had been quite important in Roman times, but had fallen away during the Anglo-Saxon years. Henry I re-established it in the early twelfth century – he built a residence, even spending Christmas there in 1122, and in 1130 the Pipe Rolls record that a steward was to be paid a penny a day to look after the property when the King was away. Henry also issued a proclamation inviting people to rent an acre of land, effectively establishing Dunstable as a borough, with a framework for rents and trading, and for the operation of the law. Later, he established a new Priory – the Priory House, which served as a guest house for travellers in the medieval period, survives as the modern visitor centre.

On the economic side, Dunstable specialised in wool, certainly by the thirteenth century. A group of local merchants were granted licences to buy fleeces from local farmers and export them. Some of these men were also producers, in villages like Caddington and Kensworth, either side of Watling Street to the south of the town. One can imagine the road busy with carts with recently sheared wool, or possibly sheep on the hoof, heading north into town, meeting the assembled consignments of fleeces heading south for London and the Continent. In the centre of the town itself, you can still see where the main road widens out into the marketplace, just south of the crossroads between Watling Street and the equally ancient Icknield Way (now known, more prosaically, as High Street South and West Street). A modern market cross marks the spot where the cattle market took place until 1958, near to Middle Row, where the earthy scent of the cows mingled with the exotic whiff of spices and maybe sweet-smelling potions.

Shrewsbury grew to greater prominence in the late Middle Ages, also on the back of the wool trade. The medieval street pattern is still discernible, and the surviving street names help us to understand not just what trades took place but how the area would have looked and felt: Butcher Row with carcasses hanging up, the distinctive smell of Fish Street, and the more sleazy activities going on in Grope Lane – this meant what it suggests, and is a rare survivor, since most roads carrying this name have been cleaned up and renamed Grove Lane!

In between those two towns, Coventry also developed thanks to the wool trade, and became the fourth largest town in England

Figure 13 Dunstable marketplace alongside the main road

by 1400. Economists and Treasury officials (including me when I worked there) continue to debate the effectiveness of tax breaks in encouraging business, but it's a practice which goes back a long way. Earl Ranulf II granted a new borough charter to Coventry in the 1150s, which gave newcomers a year's freedom from tax provided they built some new houses. Whatever the short-run effect, the powerful guilds introduced more restrictions, and 'entrepreneurs' took their business elsewhere – rather as today's sceptics about tax incentives suspect.[4]

A particular type of trader was the individual who decided to hit the road to make his or her fortune. We know less of them than of the deeds of kings and nobles, but some have passed into legend. The Holyhead road out of London features in pantomimes all over the country every Christmas, in the story of Dick Whittington.

---

[4] Hooke, 2006.

Dick was a poor boy from Gloucestershire, who came to London to make his fortune. Things did not start well for him, and he set off for home again. As he went up Highgate Hill, accompanied by his cat, he heard the sound of Bow Bells, telling him: 'Turn again, Whittington', with the added message that he would be Lord Mayor of London three times. So he turned round, and did indeed make his fortune, and become Lord Mayor.

It's a nice story, but apart from the fact that there was a Richard Whittington, who was Lord Mayor four times in the late fourteenth and early fifteenth centuries, there is no real basis for it. It has, however, left a lasting imprint on the road, which passes the Whittington Hospital, and a statue of the cat.

Figure 14 Dick Whittington's cat

The distances travelled varied according to the goods and the locality. Transporting bulky farm produce by road was tricky, but even so, most rural markets relied on this rather than the rivers. According to the Bracton legal treatise, compiled between 1235 and 1259, the limit for 'short-haul marketing' was six and two-thirds of a mile, which was allegedly the maximum distance, to allow traders to travel from home and back in a day. But there is evidence of longer journeys being undertaken, if buyers were prepared to pay the price, and if the weather didn't stand in the way: some supplies came into London over distances of up to twenty miles.[5]

Trade in livestock could operate over much longer distances. By the fifteenth century, Welsh cattle drovers were driving their herds for many a long day to join local graziers at fairs in Birmingham and Coventry.[6] Others from north Wales chose to travel via Wrexham and Newport to join Watling Street east of Shrewsbury and then follow it to High Cross, before heading for Northampton. Another route, known as the 'Welsh Road', peeled off from Watling Street at Brownhills, and went via Kenilworth and Buckingham to rejoin Watling Street at Dunstable.[7]

By the middle of the fifteenth century, other goods were also being traded over a long distance. Coventry received woad as a dye for its blue cloth from Southampton, with deliveries by cart more than once a week, and sent cloth and wool in the opposite direction. The carts took three to four days to cover the 130 miles.[8]

One factor governing how far people could travel was, of course, the state of the roads themselves. The new and more direct route from Northamptonshire to Shropshire, through the heart of the West Midlands, connected up the emerging towns, and as it

[5] Britnell, 1996.
[6] Britnell, 1996.
[7] Hindle, 1973.
[8] Barker and Savage, 1974.

became more established, no doubt gave a boost to their fortunes.
There is no evidence that the medieval period saw systematic road
building. A lot of attention, however, was paid to the building of
bridges. Fording rivers could be a dangerous business – a fifteenth-
century poem commented:

> Another blessed business is bridges to make
> In places uncrossable after great showers
> What a pity to pull a dead body out of a lake
> Who was baptised in a stone font, a fellow of ours.[9]

Most of the bridge-building took place before 1250: the main
study estimates that there were almost as many bridges in 1250
as in 1750. After 1100, they tended to be built in stone instead of
timber. On the Holyhead road, there were bridges across the Severn
at both Atcham and Shrewsbury by 1200. In Shrewsbury, charter
evidence from 1121 refers to two bridges in the town (presumably
the English and Welsh). The bridge at Atcham replaced a ferry,
which had been in the hands of the Abbot of Lilleshall, and the
Abbot duly decided to put a toll on the new bridge. According
to court records, 'By common consent of Lord William fitz Alan
(sheriff of Shropshire in the late twelfth century) and other
magnates, it was provided that the abbot should make a bridge
there and take from every loaded cart belonging to Shrewsbury 1d
and from others ½d.'[10]

At least some efforts were also made to ensure that bridges were
maintained. Stony Stratford and Fenny Stratford were both indeed
originally fords: Stony Stratford denotes the place where a Roman
road ('strat') forded the Great Ouse (the first major river crossing
out of London), with stones on the bed of the ford, as distinct
from Fenny Stratford, meaning 'marshy ford'. As early as 1254,

---

[9] Quoted in Harrison, 2004.
[10] Quoted in Harrison, 2004.

Hugh de Vere, Earl of Oxford, paid half a mark for bridge vigil in Stony Stratford.[11] By the fourteenth century, the authorities made grants of 'pontage', meaning the right to collect a toll to maintain a bridge, either to named individuals or to local people as a group. There were numerous grants in Shrewsbury, and some further east in the Shifnal area, and in Nuneaton.[12] Back in the Stratfords, the Patent Rolls tell us that in 1383, a grant of pontage was made to Richard Candeler and Geoffrey Hall of Fenny Stratford. In 1401, the grant was made to the 'good men of the town'.[13]

Fixing the bridges, of course, did nothing for the state of the roadway itself, which could be a serious problem. In busy areas, the carriageway suffered from the loading of cartwheels and horses' hooves – the effect must have been similar to what happens today when a woodland track is chewed up after rain by a logging vehicle and a few horses, leaving deep ruts and mud. Then, as now, users were keener on having the road maintained than on paying for it. By 1285, King Edward I felt moved to write to the Prior of Dunstable, demanding better maintenance of the road, with thinly veiled threats of what would happen if action was not taken:

> We have understood that the high roads which go through the centre of your town are so broken and deep because of the frequent passage of carts that dangerous injuries constantly threaten those who pass along these roads: [...] we instruct you, that is each one according to his situation and resources, to have those roads filled in and repaired [...] so that we are not obliged to take stricter measures in this regard through your default.[14]

---

[11] Victoria County History, *A History of the County of Buckinghamshire: Volume 4* (ed. William Page, 1927), at British History Online.

[12] Cooper, 2006.

[13] Victoria County History, *A History of the County of Buckinghamshire: Volume 4* (ed. William Page, 1927), at British History Online.

[14] *Annals of Dunstable Priory*, quoted in Roucoux, 1984.

There is some later evidence of repairs taking place, up and down the road. The town of Atherstone in Warwickshire petitioned the King for a grant of 'pavage' (similar to pontage) in 1343, because its marketplace was damp, and thus attracted few merchants.[15] In 1391 a similar grant was issued for four years to repair the King's Highway between the two Stratfords.[16] Other methods applied elsewhere. Between Smithfield and Highgate in London, William Phelipp was given Royal Licence to buy 'wood, sand and other things necessary' to fix a road that was 'muddy and worn down'. He tackled the problem by laying branches or planks across the wet areas, and filling potholes with sand.

As well as the state of the carriageway itself, the buildings alongside had a bearing on ease of travel. In Dunstable, for instance, a goldsmith applied for permission to build a shop in what is now High Street North. This was granted by the Archdeacon, on the basis that he ensured that neither his windows nor his doors obstructed travellers, whether on horseback or in carts.[17]

Alongside trade, pilgrimage was one of the main reasons for travelling in the medieval period. People had different reasons for going on pilgrimages, as Chaucer brings out. Although some of the celebrated journeys were major international trips to Jerusalem or Rome, much of the traffic was local. The religious purpose might be voluntary – seeking an indulgence in preparation for whatever lay ahead in the next world – or forced, for those in penitence for their sins in this world. For others, the journey would provide excitement and adventure at a time when many people never ventured more than a few miles from their home village.

---

[15] Cooper, 2006.
[16] General History of Stony Stratford on www.mkheritage.co.uk.
[17] www.medievaldunstable.org.uk.

Some pilgrims were well off, and would give alms to those they met on the way; others were all too happy to take those alms. Since pilgrimage journeys could be dangerous, the pilgrims often travelled in groups for safety.

The scale of pilgrimage had an important influence on the development of St Albans. The Abbey Church was rebuilt in the early twelfth century, and re-consecrated in 1115, using a lot of stone and brick from the decaying Roman settlement down the hill in Verulamium, to become what was then one of the largest churches in the world. It's an imposing sight today, coming into view on its hill some miles away, as you approach heading south from Redbourn, for instance. It must have been all the more striking and inspiring for medieval travellers.

You can still trace the route which the pilgrims followed, through the town and down to a door on the north side of the cathedral, which took them fairly directly to the shrine housing the relics of Saint Alban. Overlooking the shrine is the watching chamber, built in wood in about 1400 and the only one in England, where a monk sat watching over the pilgrims as they said their prayers. It's interesting to reflect on their emotions. For the monk, it was part of his daily routine. For the pilgrims, it was at the very least an important point within a journey, both physical and spiritual, and for many the culmination of that journey. Some would have been forced into pilgrimage, to atone for a particular sin – they might be outwardly observant, but privately glad that they could now go home, with the slate wiped clean. But for the truly devout, reaching the shrine could be the culmination of their spiritual life: a chance to get closer to God by venerating the relics of the martyr, in a way that would sustain them for many years to come.

Whatever their reasons, a souvenir industry developed to meet their needs: St Albans museum has a pewter badge from the fourteenth century, depicting the Saint's martyrdom.

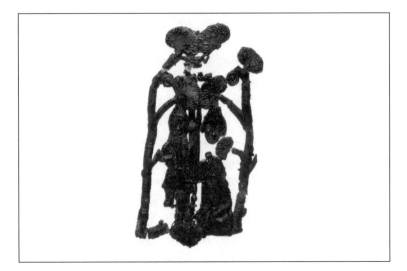

Figure 15 A pilgrim badge from St Albans

The tradition continues. Each year, on the Saturday nearest St Alban's day on 22 June, hundreds of pilgrims pour into St Albans on the Alban Pilgrimage – I've been myself (though not a worshipper), walking with a group from my wife's church from the outskirts of London to the heart of the city. The story of Alban is re-enacted using giant puppets. The cathedral is full for the Festival Evensong, so you don't get to approach the shrine in the traditional way, but you do get a sense of how the city was taken over by pilgrims at busy times. The Archbishop of Canterbury, Justin Welby, preached at the 2015 event.

Just as the motives of the pilgrims varied, so too did those of the adherents of churches and cathedrals. The monks and abbots will have wanted to ensure a proper religious experience for their visitors. But these also represented an important source of income. Some pilgrims, at least, had a choice about which shrine to visit, so there developed an element of competition among pilgrimage centres, and hence a need to refresh the offering. After Canterbury sprang up as an alternative venue following the martyrdom of St Thomas a Becket in 1170, St Albans Abbey made the mysterious discovery of the relics of Amphibalus, who had been sheltered by St Alban, at nearby Redbourn in 1178. A century later, the original mausoleum of St Alban himself emerged, in 1256–57, prompting a pilgrimage visit from the Archbishop of York.[18]

Accommodating all the visitors was well beyond the resources of the abbey guesthouse, even after a new hall was built in the mid-thirteenth century, so increasing the numbers of inns that sprang up. By 1484, the pressure was such that the Abbot gave the landlord of the George, Thomas Hethnes, permission to have Mass said in the inn if there was a chaplain present with the pilgrims.

Lichfield remained the other main pilgrim site on Watling Street. By the end of the twelfth century, it was clear that the cathedral was too small to receive the number of pilgrims coming to visit St Chad's shrine, and building started on a new Gothic cathedral, though it was not completed until the 1330s. In 1300, Bishop Walter de Langton, treasurer to Edward I, purchased a gold shrine to contain the bones of St Chad for the then astronomical price of £2000. He may have seen this partly as an investment, since it increased the flow of pilgrims and thus the prosperity of the city. Later visitors included King Richard II, who first came in 1397 and took a keen interest for the remaining two years of his reign.

Shrewsbury also boasted a shrine, to St Winifred. This was visited by Henry V, among others.[19]

Pilgrims were not universally welcomed, partly becuse they were not always all they seemed to be. Richard II and Edward IV passed laws against beggars who posed as pilgrims.[20]

[18] Webb, 2000.
[19] Ibid.
[20] Ibid.

An anonymous voice from the reform-minded religious movement known as the Lollards went further:

> Commonly such pilgrimages maintain lechery, gluttony, drunkenness, extortions, wrongs and worldly vanities. For men who may not practise their lechery at home […] make plans many days in advance and collect what funds and supplies they can, pinching and scraping to do so, to go out of the country on pilgrimage to distant images. On the way they live in lechery, in gluttony, in drunkenness, and maintain the falseness of landlords, cooks and taverners[21]

It's certainly the case that inns also developed outside the main pilgrimage sites. The Berwyn Arms in Glyndyfrdwy dates itself back to 1359; and the half-timbered Old Crown in Digbeth, a mile or so from the centre of Birmingham, originated in 1368, and says that it has 'seen off Civil War soldiers, Victorian town planners, German bombs, and a few centuries worth of drunk Brummies'. Its well is thought to have been sunk over 1000 years ago. Further south, the Cock Inn in Kilburn was licensed in 1486.

As well as trade and pilgrimage, governance was an important reason for travel. The road connected a monarch and his people, and kings and their retinues were familiar travellers along Watling Street. Personal visibility was important in establishing and reinforcing authority. St Albans was a particularly popular destination: as well as being close to London, the abbey became increasingly influential through its scholarship and its wealth. King John went there shortly after his coronation, and subsequently, to show both piety and conformity with an English tradition. Matthew Paris records that John's son, Henry III, visited on several occasions, and donated gold rings and cloth hangings to the abbey.

---

[21] Quoted in Brown, 1994.

Edward I was a regular visitor to Dunstable, sometimes making presents to the priory, sometimes dispensing justice in tricky cases.[22] He also stopped in St Albans in 1299 en route to fight the Scots, commenting:

> I have come devoutly hither for this reason, to seek licence and aid of the glorious martyr Alban and humbly to beg from this convent and people the benefit of their prayers. I must go to Scotland to suppress the arrogant presumption of my enemies the Scots, and I have no idea whether I shall succeed or whether I shall return.

In the event, Edward was back in good time to spend Easter 1300 in St Albans.[23]

King Edward's reference to the Scots highlights that conflict continued to have its impact on Watling Street. Castles and fortifications were in place from St Albans to the Welsh border, and still dominate the landscape in, for example, Tamworth and Oswestry. The area to the west of Shrewsbury was particularly well provided with castles to help guard this area along the border with Wales known as the Marches – the remnants survive in Shrawardine and West Felton. Driving or walking through the area today, it appears very peaceful, but this was far from the case in the medieval period.

The first serious threat from the Welsh arose in the 1160s, prompting Henry II to gather an army at Shrewsbury in 1164, which marched through Oswestry and into Wales towards Corwen along the route known then as 'the English Road', before suffering reversals in the hills south of Llangollen and retreating.[24] A more

[22] www.medievaldunstable.org.uk.
[23] Webb, 2000; see also Victoria County History, *A History of the County of Hertford: Volume 2*, in British History Online.
[24] Warren, 1973.

serious challenge arose at the end of the next century, in the early years of Henry IV's reign.

Owain Glyndwr, a landowner in the Dee valley, had capitalised on a number of personal and wider grievances to launch a rebellion against the King, formally taking up an ancestral title of Prince of Powys in September 1400 in Corwen. Within a year, he had established his authority over much of north and mid-Wales. In 1403, Glyndwr was joined by two former allies of the King, the Earl of Northumberland and his son Henry Hotspur, and the King headed north and west to meet them.

Shakespeare gives us a picture of life among the King's troops, as they make their way along Watling Street. Among the officers was the doughty Sir John Falstaff, who shows his characteristic set of priorities:

> Bardolph, get thee before to Coventry; fill me a bottle of sack [wine]: our soldiers shall march through: we'll to Sutton Coldfield tonight.

His troops were clearly not kitted out for the journey ahead...

> There is but a shirt and a half in all my company [...] and the shirt, to say the truth, stolen from my host at St Albans, or the red-nose innkeeper of Daventry.[25]

The King's forces prevailed when the opposing troops engaged with each other near Shrewsbury, and Hotspur was killed. Glyndwyr continued to be a thorn in the King's side for a few years, with Henry choosing to invade from Ireland to suppress Welsh forces in Anglesey, and more raids taking place in the Midlands, until Glyndwyr gradually lost power and went into hiding after 1412. He is believed to have died around 1416, and is commemorated with a fine statue right on the A5 in the middle of Corwen, all in black,

---

[25] *Henry IV, Part I*, Act 4, Scene 2.

Figure 16 Statue of Owain Glyndwyr, Corwen

mounted on his horse, with his sword held high ready to strike his foes. No wonder Henry had difficulty keeping him under control.

Half a century later, St Albans witnessed two major battles in the Wars of the Roses. King Henry VI had recovered from a period of illness, and sought to strengthen his authority by holding a great council at Leicester. The Yorkists marched against him, and the forces met at St Albans in May 1455, with the Yorkists emerging victorious, capturing the King and taking him back to London with them. Again Shakespeare tells the story – the last Act of *Henry VI, Part II* takes place in St Albans. Earlier in the play, a wizard called Roger Bolingbrook had raised a spirit which predicted that the Duke of Somerset would die 'where castles mounted stand'. Somerset met his end near the Castle Inn (a bit of a stretch?), and the Duke of York duly gloats over his body:

> So lie thou there:
> For underneath an ale-house' paltry sign,
> The Castle in St Albans, Somerset
> Hath made the wizard famous in his death

The site of the alehouse is now a building society, but a blue plaque marks Somerset's death.

Six years later, the forces locked horns again at St Albans. The Earl of Warwick, a Yorkist ally, drew up his troops on Watling Street to the north of the town, aiming to see off the Lancastrian forces led by Queen Margaret, who were heading south. She captured Dunstable on 16 February 1461 and got the better of the battle at St Albans the next day, though their dominance overall was short-lived.

After some relatively peaceful years, fighting resumed and again Watling Street found itself at the centre of events, this time further south at Barnet, a battle won by the Yorkist King Edward IV. In *Henry VI, Part III*, Warwick and King Edward IV meet in Coventry: clearly preparing for a journey down Watling Street, Warwick says:

> I will away towards Barnet presently,
> And bid thee battle, Edward, if thou dar'st.

Edward did indeed dare, and prevailed on that occasion. Soon after his death, in 1483, his teenage son, now Edward V, was travelling from Ludlow in Shropshire towards London, and spent the night in Stony Stratford, at the then Rose and Crown inn.[26] There he met his newly appointed guardian, his uncle Richard, Duke of Gloucester. Richard dispatched Edward's previous advisers, and took him, presumably down Watling Street, to the Tower of London. He never re-emerged, and it is widely believed that he and his brother were murdered by Richard, becoming known as the two 'Princes in the Tower'.

The final battle of the Wars of the Roses, at Bosworth Field, also has links to Watling Street. The Duke of Gloucester, now Richard III, faced Henry Tudor. After landing in Wales in early August 1485, Henry made first for Shrewsbury, seeking to gather support as he went. He then headed east, broadly along Watling Street, camping at Lichfield on 19 August. Still trying to boost his resources, Henry met the influential Stanley family at Atherstone in Warwickshire – a discussion which paid off in the end, after the Stanleys came down on Henry's side at a late stage of the battle.

The year 1485 is conventionally seen as a landmark in English history: the end of the medieval period and the start of the Tudor century. But most of the journeys along the Holyhead road will have continued as before. The same applies to a particular kind of trip which began in the medieval period and carried on long after it. Like his predecessors, Henry had to face down a number of armed rebellions, and one of the claimants to the throne, Perkin Warbeck, took his last journey on earth to be hung from the Tyburn tree in 1499. Since 1196, London's convicted felons had met their end at this point at the southernmost point of the Roman Watling Street, very near today's Marble Arch. In those days, the 'Tyburn tree' was indeed a tree, or one of a row of elms – not until 1571 did there

[26] http://www.mkheritage.co.uk/mkm/stonystratford.

exist an actual gallows. Warbeck may have been one of the best-known victims: he was far from being the first or last.

So although 1485 was important in dynastic terms, it did not mark an immediate and dramatic change in the wider life of the country. For parts of the Holyhead road, the landscape was changed more by decisions about the governance of the Church taken by Henry's son forty years later.

Chapter 5

Trade, Plots and Civil War: The Road Between 1500 and 1700

For amending of highways, being now very noisome and tedious to travel in and dangerous to all passengers and carriages; Be it enacted [...] that the constables and churchwardens of every parish within this realm shall yearly, upon the Tuesday or Wednesday in Easter week, call together a number of the parochians and shall then elect and choose two honest persons of the parish to be surveyors and orderers for one year of the works for amendment of the highways in their parish leading to any market town...

—'An Act for the Amending of Highways', 1555

In 1533, dignitaries travelled along the Holyhead road to play their part in a controversy of a very different kind from the armed battles of the previous century, and one that was arguably even more significant.

On 8 May of that year, a court began work in the Lady Chapel of Dunstable Priory, presided over by the Archbishop of Canterbury, Thomas Cranmer. Its job was to consider the annulment of the marriage of Henry VIII and Catherine of Aragon, and Dunstable was chosen because Catherine was living not far away at Ampthill, though she chose not to attend the court. After a fortnight or so, Cranmer announced the conclusion: that the marriage was null and void. Anne Boleyn was crowned Queen just over a week later, and the process which led to the English Reformation was a stage further on.

Dunstable Priory today seems an unlikely venue for such a genuinely momentous decision. Not only is it away from the centres of power, either religious or secular, but it is more like a handsome parish church than a seat for a historic court hearing. The explanation for that lies with one of the second-round consequences of the annulment. By the end of the decade, Henry had dissolved abbeys and monasteries up and down the country, including Dunstable. In the medieval period, the Priory had been a regional centre of learning and worship, with extensive buildings and wealth. Over time, most of the once splendid buildings fell into disuse and had to be taken down, leaving us with the church we see today.

A further product of Henry's decision was the first eyewitness account of the road and many places along it. On the King's behalf, a scholar and poet named John Leland travelled the country in the 1530s, visiting monasteries and other religious houses to check on the books in their libraries. These journeys seem to have instilled an enjoyment of travelling as an end in itself: between 1539 and 1543, he made a series of tours through England and Wales, capturing his impressions in a series of 'itineraries'. In a letter to Henry in the mid-1540s, he summed up his labours:

> I have so travelid yn yowr dominions booth by the se costes and the midle partes, sparing nother labor nor costes, by the space of these vi. yeres paste, that there is almoste nother cape, nor bay, haven, creke or peere, river or confluence of rivers, breches, waschis, lakes, meres, fenny waters, montaynes, valleis, mores, hethes, forestes, wooddes, cities, burges, castelles, principale manor placis, monasteries, and colleges, but I have seene them; and notid yn so doing a hole worlde of thinges very memorable.

Leland's text has a real sense of discovery, of someone often finding out about parts of his country for the first time. His earlier interest in books was matched by an interest in the world around him – springs, rivers, parks and the lie of the land are all covered.

Leland roams around in his journey through the Midlands, using both the old Roman Watling Street route and the more direct route to London through Coventry. As he heads north, his first direct mention of the road comes at Markyate, which he describes as 'a straggling roadside settlement along Watling Street, with modest houses reasonably built'.[1] He says a bit more when he reaches Weedon Bec in Northamptonshire:

> Weedon is a pleasant roadside place, on a level site, and is well known to carriers because it stands next to the famous road, which is commonly known by the local people as Watling Street. On this account, the place is called Weedon on the Street.

Further on, he notes the road's continuing role as a boundary:

> In the direction of Rugby, the boundary with Leicestershire runs along Watling Street.

The importance of bridges emerges clearly. He finds Coleshill, north-east of Birmingham, 'an attractive roadside town' whose bridge 'has stone arches'. In Shropshire, he finds 'a fine stone bridge over the Severn four miles above Shrewsbury called Montford Bridge and it has recently been renewed [and] A fine long bridge of stone […] at Atcham'.

Leland is more interested in the topography than in economic analysis, but gives some insights into how the country is developing, after a few decades of peace following the civil wars of the previous century. He likes Coventry, but worries about its economic future:

---

[1] All quotations are taken from John Chandler's 1993 edition of *Itinerary*, Leland, 1993.

There are many fine streets of good timber buildings [...] The town grew because of its cloth and cap manufacturing industry, but now these are in decline, Coventry's glory is waning.

Birmingham felt more positive:

It is a good market town [...] so far as I could see it has only one parish church. In the town are many smiths who make knives and all kinds of cutting tools for a living, also many lorimers who make bits, and a great many nailers.

These businesses clearly depended on transport links, whether by river or road, since 'They receive their iron from Staffordshire and Warwickshire, and their coal'.

Visiting Shrewsbury, he makes a diligent record of the bridges, gates, parish churches, and religious houses, and then moves on to Oswestry through country which is 'flat and produces good corn and grass crops'. The town pleases him:

St Oswald's church is a very fine building [...] The houses are built of timber and roofed with slate. Its main livelihood is derived from selling cloth made in Wales.

There, frustratingly, we leave him, since although he did travel in Wales, he was less systematic in writing about his experiences there.

The Dissolution of the Monasteries had its impact on the roads. Fewer people went on pilgrimages, and the fall in traffic hit Shrewsbury, St Albans, and Lichfield. St Albans Abbey was already less powerful than at its height, and the dissolution cemented that trend, giving the townspeople control over their own affairs. The abbey buildings in Shrewsbury also decayed, until – admittedly nearly 300 years later – Thomas Telford was able to drive the new, straighter course of the Holyhead road through the old grounds without having to take down much if any masonry, though there are still relics of the medieval buildings on the far side of the road from the abbey.

As pilgrimage fell away, commerce picked up. Shrewsbury may have suffered from the dissolution, but it benefited from the growth in trade during the sixteenth century – particularly from the revival in the wool trade from the 1560s. The sheer number of people coming to market led to complaints from residents that the road to the Stone Bridge, now the English Bridge, was being worn away.

This popularity meant that Shrewsbury ran not one but several markets. A new market hall was built in 1595–96: the ground floor housed the market for corn, and the upper floor was used by the local drapers for the purchase of woollen cloth brought on ponies from north Wales. Meanwhile, traders in dairy produce and pigs gathered around the High Cross, while purveyors of fruit and vegetables set up their stalls elsewhere in the Cornmarket. Shopkeepers with a more permanent presence established or re-established themselves in particular streets. Butchers now began to gather, paradoxically,

Figure 17 Shrewsbury market hall

in or near Fish Street. As trade grew, the corporation added a row of upper chambers to their stalls – and put the rent up – with the street later becoming known, more logically, as Double Butcher Row.[2]

The state of the road itself may have deteriorated, but the resulting prosperity was reflected in new buildings still around today. Many successful merchants or professional men used their new wealth to build houses in the town centre, which were decorated in an ornate way, including grotesque heads and beams carved with vine trails. Mouldings to timbers and also plasterwork were used inside the houses too. Thomas Churchyard, returning to his native town after some time away, observed that there were new buildings 'gay and gallant finely wrought' whereas others 'were fat within, that outward looked leane'.[3]

Other places along the road also benefited from increased activity. Dunstable, for example, saw portable market stalls replaced by permanent workshops in Middle Row, parts of which can still be seen today. Grammar schools were founded in both Coleshill and Wolverhampton in the early sixteenth century – some of my classmates at junior school went to what was still Coleshill Grammar School in those days. Further west, Shrewsbury School followed in the middle of the century, also originally a grammar school.

This commercial development did not, however, result from improvements in the infrastructure. The system of major roads changed little over the period. The roads shown on the maps drawn by John Ogilby in the late seventeenth century are basically the same roads evidenced by the Gough Map from the late fourteenth century. As we have seen, most major bridges were actually in place by 1250, and were made of stone rather than wood by about 1500.[4]

---

[2] Champion, 2006.
[3] Ibid.
[4] Harrison, 2004

Figure 18 Tudor market place buildings, Dunstable

There were, however, repeated and more urgent efforts to improve the maintenance of the highways starting with an Act of 1531 focusing on bridges. The initial problem was working out who was responsible for their upkeep in the first place. As the Act said:

> in many parts of this realm, it cannot be known and proved, what Hundred, Riding, Wapentake, City, Borough, Town, or Parish, nor what person certain or body politic ought of right to make such bridges decayed, by reason whereof such decayed bridges [...] lie long without any amendment, to the great annoyance of the King's Subjects.

The Statute therefore provided that Justices of the Peace would:

> enquire, hear and determine ... all manner of anoysances of bridges broken in the highways to the damage of the King's liege people.

In terms of action, the Act gave JPs:

> power and authority to tax and set every Inhabitant […] to
> such reasonable aid and sum of money as they shall think by
> their discretions convenient and sufficient for the repairing,
> re-edefying and amendment of such bridges.[5]

In 1555, the government of Queen Mary, more associated with the re-establishment of Catholicism than with transport policy, took a Highways Act through Parliament, which placed responsibility for road maintenance on local parishes – prior to this, it had rested loosely with landowners. Each parish was required to elect 'two honest persons' to fill the newly created role of Surveyor of Highways, with the unenviable task of corralling their fellow parishioners into four eight-hour days of hard work 'for amendment of the highways in their parish leading to any market town'. On top of that, people owning or working land had to supply 'one wain or cart furnished after the custom of the country, with oxen, horses, or other cattle, and all other necessaries meet to carry things convenient for that purpose, and also two able men with the same'. Every cottager or labourer had themselves to 'work and travail in the amendment of the said highways'. And they had to provide their own tools for the job:

> every person and carriage abovesaid [sic]shall have and bring
> with them such shovels, spades, picks, mattocks, and other tools
> and instruments as they do make their own ditches and fences
> withal…[6]

The Act also showed a touching faith in the capacity of the sun to maintain the roads in England: it requires the surveyors to keep roadways clear and hedges trimmed, so that the sun will dry the

---

[5] Statute of Bridges, 1531, quoted in Tanner, 1951, and Cooper, 2006.
[6] *An Act for the amending of Highways*, quoted in Tanner, 1951.

roads and allow them 'to grow better of themselves'.[7] Having poked fun at this sixteenth-century approach, it's only fair to add that no less an expert than Thomas Telford also took advantage of the sun when he rebuilt the road in the 1820s: he positioned lay-bys on the north side of the new road in Wales, to store materials to maintain the road, so that the sun would help to dry them. You can still see some of these lay-bys today.

Perhaps not surprisingly, the Tudor legislation did not completely succeed in ensuring effective upkeep of the roads, and Parliament had to return to the issue regularly. As early as 1562, the time commitment was increased from four days to six, and surveyors were given extra powers to remove rubbish from roads, and acquire stone for repairs. In 1575, a new Act required a greater contribution from landowners.

The statute labour approach was difficult to enforce, and pressure on the road system was growing as more wheeled vehicles, increasingly four-wheelers, took to the highways as the economy developed. So by 1621, measures of a different sort were taken to relieve pressure, with a proclamation limiting the weight of wagons to 1 ton, but that was not wholly effective either, and the search for new approaches went on.

After 1660, attention switched to turnpike trusts as a way of maintaining the roads: the idea that a group of people could be given the right to charge a toll for using a stretch of road, in return for keeping it in good order. A Parliamentary committee was set up in 1664 to look at ways of improving the roads, and 'in particular take into consideration the repairing and making the Highway from London to West Chester'. They came down in favour of a toll, but two attempts at legislation made little progress,

[7] Kind, 1999.

and, as for nearly all roads, it was only in the eighteenth century that turnpikes were introduced on the Holyhead road.[8]

Like trade, the governance of the realm required a viable transport system. In the early sixteenth century, the government started funding certain innkeepers to keep horses that officials travelling on the Crown's business could use, and which could carry the Royal Mail; the deal involved providing the men to run this as well. One example on our road may be Little Brickhill, near Milton Keynes, described by John Ogilby later as 'a post town and of good reception'.[9] The target speed for the horses was 7mph in summer and 5mph in winter. Later in the sixteenth century, this system was opened up to the wider public, for a fee, and in the 1630s a regular public mail service was established.[10]

Not everyone benefited from the growing economy, of course, and the Tudor regime was concerned not just about the maintenance of the roads but about the number of poor people wandering along them. Rich and poor shared one set of roads, so there was no hiding from the impact. Cardinal Wolsey instigated campaigns against the wandering and mendicant poor in Coventry and Shrewsbury, among other places, between 1517 and 1521.

For many vagrants, there was a pattern to their activity, following the seasons. In March, they would hit the road in search of work, and some would travel quite a distance – about half in one study had travelled more than forty miles, and nearly a quarter more than 100 miles. By October, they were hunkering down again. They often knew the roads well, and while most walked, they might also go on horseback or in a cart. Then as now, London acted as a magnet for people in search of work, and there was particular concern about vagrancy in Hertfordshire and other counties near the capital.

---

[8] Pawson, 1977.
[9] Ogilby, ed. Harley, 1970.
[10] Barker and Savage, 1974.

Many of the towns on the Holyhead road hosted fairs that attracted the wayfarers, including Nuneaton in the 1580s, where a woman reported that 'there were minstrels playing and there they made good cheer'.[11] Others moved around within a region: there is an example of a seamstress who travelled from market to market in the Marches, 'to get a penny to help to maintain her', visiting Wellington and Oswestry before being arrested in Shrewsbury.

Others regarded as undesirable included highway robbers. The wooded and undulating landscape of Nesscliffe Hill, north of Shrewsbury, became a notorious meeting place for them. The best-known was 'Wild Humphrey Kynaston', reputed to be a Robin Hood figure, who was outlawed for his part in a murder, and lived

Figure 19 Kynaston's cave, Nesscliffe Hill

[11] Slack, 1988, and Beier, 1985.

in a cave on the hillside for some time. He was pardoned in 1516 and died peacefully in 1534. Nowadays, his cave is a home for rare bats, including Daubenton's and Natterer's.

The growing prosperity, at least for some, may have reflected the peace which existed at home, if not abroad, through the Tudor period, in place of the battles and troop movements of the previous centuries. There were, of course, plots against the established order, and the most famous of them all, the Gunpowder Plot of 1605, involved a dash up the Holyhead road.

Much of the planning had taken place in the Manor House at Ashby St Ledgers in Northamptonshire, which was owned by the leading conspirator, Robert Catesby. On the eve of the planned explosion, one of the conspirators, Sir Everard Digby, was stationed at Dunchurch, poised to capture King James's daughter, Elizabeth, and put her on the throne in place of her father. Once Guy Fawkes was discovered and arrested, most of the other conspirators fled north to join Digby. The last to set off, but the fastest, was Ambrose Rookwood, who covered thirty miles in two hours, to meet three of his fellows at Little Brickhill, and then to join Catesby and others further north as they headed to Dunchurch. Their flight continued into Staffordshire, but ended soon afterwards.

They and other plotters failed to disturb a long spell of peace, but this finally came to an end with the outbreak of the Civil War in 1642. Unlike in the Wars of the Roses, none of the main battles took place on the Holyhead road itself, but there was plenty of activity up, down and across it.

In the immediate run-up to the war, Charles I marched on Coventry with a view to dislodging a Parliamentary force, but chose to back off. Having raised his Standard in Nottingham, he retreated to the Marches and based himself at the Council House in Shrewsbury for a few weeks, using it as a base for recruiting troops.

The Corporation strengthened the town defences, including fortifying two key bridges carrying the Holyhead road either side of the town, at Atcham and Montford. Shrewsbury remained a Royalist stronghold, but the pressure intensified as Parliament obtained the upper hand in the War: they captured Oswestry in 1644, and Shrewsbury itself in February 1645.

Birmingham had seen some action earlier in the War. In 1642, suspected Royalist sympathisers were rounded up and sent as prisoners to Coventry, where they were not welcome – it may be that this is the origin of the expression 'sent to Coventry', meaning to ostracise someone. The following year, Prince Rupert tried to set up camp in Birmingham, but was unable to do so, according to the eighteenth-century historian, William Hutton, because 'the inhabitants had choked up, with carriages, the deep and narrow road then between Deritend and Camp Hill, which obliged the Prince to alter his route'.[12]

The Prince eventually made it through Birmingham, on his way to Lichfield. This city was in an important position, at the crossroads of Royalists' supply routes, including those from Liverpool to Oxford and Leeds to Bristol.[13] Lichfield was split: the cathedral authorities supported the King, whereas most of the townsfolk favoured the Parliamentary side. The cathedral close was fortified in 1643, and control swapped to and fro through the War, with three sieges, which meant that Lichfield suffered more damage than any other cathedral city.

As the War approached its conclusion, in June 1645, King Charles was further south along the road, in Daventry, ahead of the Battle of Naseby, staying at The Wheatsheaf Inn (which is now a care home). After his defeat at Naseby, the King

[12] Hutton, 1783.
[13] Lichfield Museum.

retreated via Lichfield and Wolverhampton towards Hereford and then Cardiff.

The remaining action near the Holyhead road came after Charles I had been beheaded, and his son, Charles II, was trying to build support against the Parliamentary government in the west of England. He was defeated at the Battle of Worcester on 3 September 1651, but staged a remarkable and notorious escape, in which he dodged around for several days in the area between the Roman Watling Street (the modern A5) and the then Holyhead road (now the A41). From Worcester, he went to White Ladies Priory on 4 September, then to Evelith Mill, near Shifnal, on the fifth, and then to Madeley (now part of Telford) and to Boscobel House, where he hid successfully in an oak tree, on the sixth, before finally making good his escape to France on the seventh.

With the end of the Civil War, regular traffic on the road picked up again. There had been a twice-weekly coach service between St Albans and London, established by John Taylor, from 1637. Twenty years on, the *Mercurius Politicus* magazine of 9 April 1657 advertised a longer and more frequent service:

> For the convenient accommodation of passengers from and betwixt London and West Chester, there is provided several stage-coaches, which go from the George Inn, without Aldersgate, upon every Monday, Wednesday, and Friday – to Coventry in two days, for 25 shillings; to Stone in 3 days, for 30 shillings; and to Chester in four days, for 35 shillings; and from thence do return upon the same days, which is performed with much ease to the passengers, having fresh horses once a day.[14]

[14] Quoted in Harper, 1902.

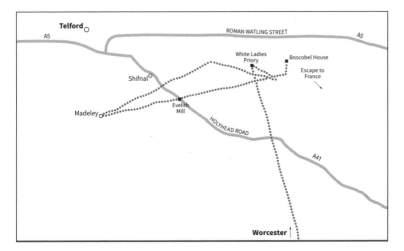

Map 2 Charles II's escape route after the Battle of Worcester

The development of such services was a major feature of the next 150 years.

Other more local journeys carried on. Tyburn remained the location for public executions, though the Tyburn tree was replaced by a proper gallows in 1571. Perhaps its most prominent customer was Oliver Cromwell, whose body was exhumed and hanged soon after the restoration of Charles II.

Samuel Pepys records in his diary that his wife witnessed those events. Pepys himself tried to visit some years later, but was thwarted:

> and so away with Mr Pierce, the surgeon, towards Tyburne (sic), to see the people executed; but came too late, it being done; two men and a woman hanged.[15]

Towards the end of the century, we have another comprehensive insight into the places along the road. John Ogilby had a varied career, but became interested in mapping after he lost his home

---

[15] Samuel Pepys's *Diary*, 23 October 1668.

in the Great Fire of London. In his *Itinerarium Angliae* of 1675, he describes himself as 'His Majesty's Cosmographer' – and, incidentally, as 'Master of His Majesty's Revels in the Kingdom of Ireland', though we don't know whether these duties took him regularly to Holyhead or not.

The *Itinerarium* is a remarkable work: if the Gough Map is the first accurate map of England, the *Itinerarium* is the first road atlas. Ogilby produces strip maps, at a scale of an inch to a mile, of eighty-five roads, with the Holyhead road prominent among them. Ogilby's observations bring out how the road had developed over the past two centuries, with some specialist markets, and a well-established network of inns. He traces the route out of London via Islington and Barnet, which he calls 'a well-frequented town, noted for its medicinal waters, good inns, and a swine-market on Monday'. St Albans is 'large and well-frequented', and 'sends stage coaches daily to London'. Dunstable 'has a good market on Wednesdays for corn and cattle, and is noted for good larks'.

He comments with interest that near Potters Perry (spelt Potterspury today), 'your road keeps straight, but somewhat woody, shewing some visible remains of the old Roman way', but then records that the main road, 'At 68'3 leaves the direct Watling-street at the Cross o'th' Hand' – 68'3 represents the mileage from London. He describes the Roman Watling Street route as 'the Street way to Watford gap'.

On his main route, Daventry pleases him with 'divers handsome inns', as does Coventry with 'the stateliest cross in the kingdom' as well as three weekly markets and four fairs each year. He skirts Birmingham to the east – in an alternative route later in the book, he calls it 'Birmingham vulgo Bromicham', 'a large and well-built town, drives a great trade in most sorts of iron work'. At Weeford, near Lichfield, he notes that 'The Watlingstreet Way you left at

Weedon ... here thwarts your road and proceeds to Shrewsbury etc'. From there, his route diverges from both Watling Street and the coaching road, going via Stone in Staffordshire to Chester, which he says, 'has a great intercourse with Ireland ... [with] a Midsummer Fair ... and another great Fair at Michaelmas, both of which are plentifully furnished and frequented by the Tradesmen of London and Dublin'.

The route then goes across north Wales to Conway and Anglesey. Crossing the Menai Strait was a well-known problem: Ogilby shows a route across sands, but marks it carefully 'when ye tide is out'! At the end of the road, he finds Holyhead 'a scattering Town consisting chiefly of Houses for Entertainment of such Persons as either are bound for Ireland or lately arrived thence'.

Ogilby's work is very different from Leland's. As well, of course, as differences in personality and interest, this reflects a shift, over about 135 years, from long-distance travel being an adventure and an exploration to something that needed a practical guide. So Ogilby provides the mileage for his Holyhead road – 269 miles. He explains the route in some detail in places – to help travellers on the tricky last stretch into Holyhead, he advises to 'observe the Right-hand Way to Cleveock Sands, leading to Holyhead when the tide is out, otherwise you proceed by Way of the bridge'. For each double page of directions, at the start he lists 'Turnings to be avoided', and at the end, 'Backward turnings to be avoided' for people heading back to London.

In the same practical vein, Ogilby produced a companion volume, *Britannia*, which provides maps at one inch to the mile for the first time, in the process setting the standard for the mile at 1760 yards. He describes the Holyhead road as 'one of the most frequented roads of the kingdom, accordingly affording good entertainment for travellers'. Precise routes varied: not all stagecoaches went via

Lichfield, and 'horsemen will sometimes ride by Northampton and carts keep the Watlingstreet'.[16] He identifies some of the inns which the traveller would come across, including the Cock and the Bell near Coney Green, the Red Lion near Hockliffe, and the Cock at Braunston (between Daventry and Dunchurch).

One traveller who may have benefited from Ogilby's work was Celia Fiennes. She was the daughter of an aristocrat, who showed plenty of courage and stamina in touring the country on horseback in the years around 1700, with a very small retinue, to see for herself what it was like and to write up her findings. Her purpose – more like that of Leland than Ogilby – is that:

> if all persons [...] would spend some of their time in Journeys to visit their native land, [...] and make observations of the pleasant prospects, good buildings, different produces and manufactures of each place [...] it would also form such an Idea of England, add much to its Glory and Esteem in our minds, and cure the evil itch of over-valuing foreign parts.[17]

Celia Fiennes doesn't travel along the Holyhead road as a journey in its own right, but encounters it many times in her roamings. She certainly appreciates its importance. Near the Wrekin, she comments:

> Here I came into the Whatling (sic) Streete which is one of the great roads of England which divided the land into so many kingdoms under the Saxons.[18]

Sometimes she finds the roads good – from Tamworth to Lichfield, for instance, she finds 'a very good way, mostly gravel, I went it [sic] in an hour', and near the Wrekin she commented that 'The roads

16 Ogilby, ed. Harley, 1970.
17 Fiennes, ed. Morris, 1995.
18 Ibid, 'My Great Journey to Newcastle and to Cornwall', 1698.

are pretty good but the miles are long'. She was less keen on the clay soils north of London:

> we came to Dunstable over a sad road called Hockley in the
> Hole [Hockliffe] as full of deep sloughs, in the winter it must
> be impassable, there is a very good pitched Causey [causeway]
> for foot people and horse that is raised up high from the road.

As well as the state of the roads, Celia Fiennes takes a close interest in the economic life of the places she visits. She sees rennet being made in Coleshill, and remarks that Coventry is 'a thriving good trading town and is very rich'. As with Ogilby, she brings out the degree of specialisation in different trades, with the road connecting these markets. In Stony Stratford, 'they make a great deal of Bonelace [...] they sit and work all along the street as thick as can be'. By contrast, in the Cannock area, things are less picturesque:

> there is also great quantities of fern ... the whole country (sic)
> are employed in cutting it up and burning it in heaps for the sake
> of the ashes.

These ashes were used for washing and scouring and 'they send much up to London'. She also describes mining in Wales and the Midlands. On her way back, she sees the road busy with traders in the Shrewsbury area:

> I went through the great fair which was just kept the day there,
> full of all sorts of things, and all the road for 10 mile at least I
> met the people and commodities going to the fair.

Celia Fiennes sometimes found the travelling difficult, and she was far from alone in this. Looking back to her era from the perspective of the 1780s, William Hutton, the historian of Birmingham, says:

We have a common observation among us, that even so late as William the Third [1688–1702], the roads were in so dangerous a state, that a man usually made his will, and took a formal farewell of his friends, before he durst venture on a journey to London; which, perhaps, was thought then, of as much consequence as a voyage to America now.[19]

There was to be plenty more discussion of the state of the roads in the following century.

[19] Hutton, 1783.

Chapter 6

Turnpikes, Coaches, and Inns: The Road in the Eighteenth Century

The memory of the Romans [...] is preserved in nothing more visible to common observation than in the remains of those noble causeways and highways, which they made through all parts of the kingdom, and which were found so needful even then, when there was not the five hundredth part of the commerce and carriage that is now. How much more valuable must these new works be though nothing to compare with those of the Romans for the firmness and duration of their work?

—Daniel Defoe[1]

The history of the road in the eighteenth century is one of constant interplay between extra travel and extra effort to maintain the highway. The road and the buildings along it reflected changes in society, and facilitated the journeys that these changes brought about. But while a new method of organising the maintenance, through turnpikes and tolls, proved more successful than any previous effort, it still came under severe strain.

We have another eyewitness account of conditions in the early eighteenth century. Daniel Defoe may be best known now as the

---

[1] Quotations are from Defoe, ed. Rogers, 1971.

author of *Robinson Crusoe*, but he had a number of other strings to his bow, and toured the country widely on horseback, sometimes on business, sometimes as a journalist, and sometimes on political missions for the leading statesmen of the day. In the 1720s, he did some more focused journeys prior to writing his *Tour through the Whole Island of Great Britain*, which was published in 1724–26. It is a unique work of reportage and insight into the economic and social life of the day, but also designed as a kind of guidebook – in Defoe's own words, 'Particularly fitted for the Reading of such as desire to Travel over the Island'.[2]

Defoe is positive about the changing life of the country:

> New foundations are always laying, new buildings always raising, highways repairing, churches and public buildings erecting, fires and other calamities happening, fortunes of families taking different turns, new trades are everyday erected, new projects enterprised, new designs laid.[3]

His route didn't travel up and down the Holyhead road as such, but he used it for parts of his journeys to and from Wales. He liked Shrewsbury, for example:

> This is indeed a beautiful, large, pleasant, populous, and rich town; full of gentry and yet full of trade too; for here too, is a great manufacture, as well of flannel as also of white broadcloth, which enriches all the country round it.

There he picks up the road heading east:

> Here I was shown a very visible and remarkable appearance of the great ancient road or way called Watling Street, which comes from London to this town, and goes on from hence to the utmost coast of Wales. ...

[2] Ibid.
[3] Ibid., preface to the Second Volume.

On this road we set out now for Lichfield [...] and I would gladly have kept to this old road, if it had been possible because I knew several remarkable places stood directly upon it. But we were obliged to make many excursions, and sometimes quit the street for a great way together.[4]

He doesn't often make observations about the state of the highway as he travels round, but writes about it in detail in an Appendix to his Second Volume. His starting point is a comment on the soil:

the soil of all the midland part of England [...] is of a deep stiff clay, or marly kind.

The Holyhead road is a case in point:

After you are past Dunstable, [...] you enter the deep clays, which are so surprisingly soft that it is perfectly frightful to travellers, and it has been the wonder of foreigners, how, considering the great numbers of carriages which are continually passing with heavy loads, these ways have been made practicable; indeed the great number of horses every year killed by the excess of labour in those heavy ways has been such a charge to the country that the new building of causeways as the Romans did of old seems to me to be a much easier expense.

Defoe traces the clays up the road 'even to Birmingham for very nearly 80 miles'. And this road really matters 'as these are counties which drive a very great trade with the city of London and with one another'. The road to London was busy with waggons bringing corn from Hertfordshire and cheese from Warwickshire. As early as 1650, contemporaries commented that 'all or most of

---

[4] Defoe, Letter 7. The first departure is to White Ladies Aston and the Boscobel oak, then to Stafford.

the London ironmongers buy all or most of their nails and petty ironwork either from Birmingham, or [...] brought from thence'.[5] The vehicles carrying these supplies had to share the highway with, among others, some energetic Welsh cattle, which trekked all the way to Barnet Fair if they first succeeded in swimming across the Menai Straits from Anglesey.[6]

No wonder the state of the carriageway was under pressure, and Defoe was among many who noted that previous arrangements for maintenance were not working:

> the roads had been ploughed so deep, and materials have been in some places so difficult to be had for repair of the roads, that all the surveyors' rates have been able to do nothing; nay the very whole country has not been able to repair them; that is to say it was a burden too great for the poor farmers; for in England it is the tenant, not the landlord, that pays the surveyor of the highways.

The difference in the eighteenth century was that a new and more effective method was found, by organising road maintenance through turnpike trusts. The idea had been debated in the previous century but now took off, and Act after Act of Parliament gave a body of named trustees the power to set up their gates and levy tolls, in return for maintaining the carriageway. Tolls differed according to how a person travelled, and – no doubt reflecting their impact on the state of the roads – animals did not come free. Travellers along the Lichfield stretch of the route from London to Chester had to pay 1d for a horse, 6d for a coach, 1s for a waggon, and ½d for a score of sheep and lambs.[7]

---

[5] Upton, 1993.

[6] Dyos and Aldcroft, 1971.

[7] Lichfield Museum. The Lichfield Turnpike Trust was set up by an Act of 1729. For the majority, now, who don't remember the pre-decimal currency days,

Travellers would no doubt have been alerted to the changes because of local discussion before the Act was passed. Once implemented, gates were set up across the road, and arrangements made to collect the toll. Some of the toll cottages are still in place today, with their distinctive bay windows, to enable the toll-keeper to see both ways before leaving his property to collect the money from the traveller and open the gate. There are some particularly fine examples on the Holyhead road in Wales, where they were built as part of Telford's improvements in the early nineteenth century.

The system took time to establish itself. The first Turnpike Act had actually been passed in 1663, setting up a trust to manage the Great North Road near Ware in Hertfordshire, but the next one did not follow until 1695. By Defoe's time, the pace was picking up: over half of the thirteen main roads out of London were turnpiked by 1730, rising to nearly 90 per cent by 1750.[8] The first turnpike on the Holyhead road was introduced in 1706, between Stony Stratford and Fornhill in Bedfordshire.[9] The road from St Albans to South Mimms was brought under a trust in 1714, and the route north to Dunstable in 1722.

The establishment of a turnpike clearly indicated that the road in question mattered: in Birmingham, the stretch of the Holyhead road heading north-west from the city centre (now actually named Holyhead Road) was turnpiked in 1727, because it was the route which brought coal from the Black Country to fuel Birmingham's furnaces.[10] Much later in the century, in 1788, the road in Deritend, near the centre of Birmingham, was turnpiked, mostly to rebuild a bridge and improve flood prevention – that was the reward for

(i.e. before 1971), 1d was an old penny, of which there were 240 to the pound, and 1s an old shilling, the equivalent of 5p.

[8] Pawson, 1977. The proportion of roads turnpiked is by mileage.

[9] Morriss, 2004.

[10] www.ramsdale.org/birmingham.

Figure 20 Boundary stone marking end of turnpike trust jurisdiction, St Albans

paying twopence for a carriage and a halfpenny for a horse. In the 1820s, coverage was extended up to Digbeth to widen a road that was under increasing pressure from the fast-growing Birmingham economy.[11]

By the middle of the century, the routes from London to Shrewsbury and Chester were virtually all in the hands of turnpikes. The route across Anglesey was turnpiked in 1765.[12] Stones were set up to mark the boundary of the trust's jurisdiction, and some can still be found, at least in museums.[13]

[11] Upton, 1993.
[12] Barker and Gerhold, 1993; Quartermaine, 2003.
[13] St Albans museum.

The turnpike system certainly improved the roads, though inevitably the impact was patchy. Turnpikes also increased spending on roads compared to the previous system of relying on the parish rate and statute labour, partly because, as well as the tolls themselves, the trusts were able to generate income by borrowing. So the trusts accounted for most of a four-fold increase in total spending on the roads between 1730, shortly after Defoe's journey, and 1800.[14] Increases in spending do not, of course, necessarily lead to commensurate improvements in service – I speak as a former Treasury official – but Defoe was certainly a supporter, particularly on Watling Street.

> Upon this great road there are wonderful improvements made and making, which no traveller can miss the observation of, especially if he knew the condition these ways were formerly in. [...] no public edifice, almshouse, hospital, or nobleman's palace, can be of equal value to the country with this, nor more an honour and ornament to it.

He finds improvements from Little Brickhill through to Stony Stratford, 'where the way was exceeding bad before'. The old road just the other side of Little Brickhill survives, by the way, but has been bypassed – I found a vantage point where I could photograph both together (see figure overleaf).

As to the precise area which had so troubled Celia Fiennes at the end of the seventeenth century:

> we now see the most dismal piece of ground for travelling, that ever was in England, handsomely repaired namely, from the top of the chalky hill beyond Dunstable down into Hockley Lane.

As a result, Defoe was optimistic about prospects further north.

[14] Bogart, 2005.

Figure 21 Little Brickhill, old and new roads side by side

> After so many encouraging examples on this great Watling
> Street road, […] they have now begun the like on the same way
> farther down […] they promise themselves that in a few years,
> those roads will be completely sound and firm, as Watling Street
> was in its most ancient and flourishing state.

The antiquarian and traveller, Thomas Pennant, writing later in the
century, also endorsed the effectiveness of turnpikes. He used the
example of another difficult stretch of road, around Meriden in
Warwickshire. The town 'got the name of Myreden; *den* signifying
a bottom and *myre*, dirt; and I can well vouch for the propriety of
the appellation before the institution of turnpikes'.[15]

Turnpikes were not a panacea, and some of the methods used
to maintain the roads could still be opportunistic. A traveller in the

---

[15] Pennant (1781).

St Albans area noted that even the ruins of Verulamium could be drawn on for materials:

Pieces of Roman brick lie thick in the road as we go to Hemsted.[16]

If the problem was manpower rather than bricks, William Hutton, who wrote a history of Birmingham, had an interesting idea. Instead of deporting convicts to the colonies, he said:

It would be easy to reduce this ferocious race under a kind of martial discipline; to badge them with a mark only removeable by the governors, for hope should ever be left for repentance, and to employ them in the rougher arts of life [...] [such as] forming canals, cleansing the beds of rivers, assisting in harvest, and in FORMING and MENDING the ROADS.[17]

The system certainly had its downsides, not least fragmentation – when he began his reforms in 1815, Telford found twenty-three separate trusts on the Holyhead road in England, and seven in Wales – and so the impact varied from place to place. Some trusts proved profitable, some were effective, some may have been both. Others did not make a difference for the better.

One reason for this was that the maintenance effort was continually struggling to keep up with the pressure exerted by the growing number of journeys on the roads.

It seems clear that agricultural production grew over the century, and that growth accelerated further after 1800, even if experts now challenge the old concept of an agricultural revolution in the eighteenth century.[18] Part of this was down to increased regional and local specialisation, implying more trade. We know that Warwickshire specialised in cheese production,

[16] St Albans museum, attributed to a writer named Salmon in 1728.
[17] Hutton, 1783. Emphasis is Hutton's.
[18] Overton, 1986.

for instance, as well as understanding which towns benefited from the wool trade.

Established merchants shifting regular cargoes did not by any means have the road to themselves – they shared it with some less sophisticated tradesmen. 'Tramping' in search of work began to be more organised from the 1740s – weavers and shoemakers were among the first to band together on the roads, partly for companionship, partly for security. Young apprentices travelled surprising distances for work, thanks in part to the system of parish apprenticeships, which meant that children from the workhouse could be sent to jobs wherever they were available – we know of a young man named Thomas Hollings of Coventry, for example, who set off along the Holyhead road in the 1770s to begin working life in south London.[19] He would have come across bands of casual labourers, entertainers, gypsies, tinkers and beggars on his way.

The much more fundamental influence was the Industrial Revolution. A few miles south of the Holyhead road, in Coalbrookdale, Abraham Darby pioneered the smelting of iron using coke in 1709. It represented a step change in the efficiency of the process, though the potential was not fully exploited until the 1750s, when Darby's son, Abraham Darby II, began producing bar iron in Ketley, where the Holyhead road ran through the north of modern Telford. And it was the end of the century before Matthew Boulton and James Watt opened the Soho Foundry in Birmingham to manufacture the steam engines they had been working on for some twenty years.

Two hundred years on, the Soho Foundry site is still used for manufacturing – at least, there were some very loud processes taking place somewhere as I stood outside the high gates. It's now a site for Avery Weigh-Tronix, which makes precision weighing machines and traces its history back to a business established in 1731 in Digbeth, a few miles back down the Holyhead road.

[19] Guldi, 2012.

Near the Foundry, also just off the Holyhead road, is Soho House, the home of Matthew Boulton from 1766 until his death in 1809, and the venue for meetings of the Lunar Society. Interestingly, the society got its name from the fact that meetings tended to be fixed for nights when the moon was full, since the state of the roads made travel in the dark hazardous.[20] One of its members was Erasmus Darwin, who would have used at least some of the Holyhead road to get to meetings from his home in Lichfield. His grandson, Charles Darwin, was born in 1809 at a house further along the road in Shrewsbury, called The Mount.[21]

As well as Soho House and the Foundry, Boulton built a 'manufactory' in that part of Birmingham, which excited admiration in *Swinney's Birmingham Directory*:

> The building consists of four Squares, with Shops, Warehouses, etc, for a thousand Workmen, who, in a great variety of Branches, excel in their several Departments; not only in the fabrication of Buttons, Buckles, Boxes, Trinkets, etc, in gold, silver, and a variety of Compositions; but in many other arts, long predominant in France.[22]

The factory set new standards in manufacturing techniques, and also in management of the staff.

By this time Birmingham had been growing rapidly for a century or so and not long after the Civil War had overtaken Coventry as the largest town in Warwickshire. A lot of the trade was in metal products, but there was a variety: toy-making, gunnery and banking all had their place. Not for nothing was Birmingham known as the 'city of a thousand trades'.

---

[20] Upton, 1993.

[21] This is another touchpoint for me, this time in my professional life: I was chief executive of the Valuation Office Agency at one point, and by historical chance, our Shrewsbury office was housed in The Mount.

[22] Upton, 1993.

Better communications enabled the growth of other towns in the Midlands. Someone writing under the name of Robert Curthose commented in the *Gentleman's Magazine* in 1787, that

> Hinckley gains fresh advantages, and seems now to rise into a more independent state of trade. The stocking manufacture, formerly subservient to two principal neighbouring towns, is at present carried on chiefly on its own account, and without the help of their medium.
>
> A mail-coach has been established to and from Chester, which passes daily through this town, besides several other regular stage-coaches from different parts. A post-office is fixed, and a postmaster appointed. Before this regulation, the letters only arrived from Coventry three times in the week; the same from Leicester, which occasioned a very great delay and detriment to business.[23]

Hinckley was to suffer something of a backlash early in the next century – it was the scene of some of the first Luddite protests against mechanisation and job losses. The reference to an 'independent state' also has echoes in the belief, at least, from locals that people from Hinckley and Nuneaton, three miles apart but on opposite sides of the main road, are reluctant to cross it to work in the other town.

The growth of Birmingham and other places as industrial centres was reflected in the growth in the number of firms whose business was to carry goods over longer distances as the road connected places increasingly far apart. Around 1700, there were maybe 400 services a week to and from London to the rest of the country. By 1767, Birmingham alone had 160 services a week, provided by more than fifty separate firms. By using larger vehicles with wider wheels, and usually a team of eight horses, they were able to carry greater weights of goods. And by changing whole teams of horses

---

[23] Quoted on the Buildings of Hinckley website.

and waggoners, they were able to move faster, sometimes running services through the night. This approach reduced the time taken to transport goods from Manchester to London from nine days to five days in the 1770s. These longer journeys took place alongside the continuing traffic from shorter hops to market towns.

Religion made a comeback as a reason for travel, though in contrast to the medieval period, it was the preachers rather than the faithful who moved. John Wesley and the Methodists were itinerant preachers, who gradually switched to operating in more defined 'circuits', a term that survives in the Methodist organisation to this day. Wesley himself travelled up and down the Midlands stretch of the road in the 1740s. An elm tree in Stony Stratford has a plaque which records that he preached there five times, apparently without incident. Sometimes, however, things were not so straightforward and he faced mobs who objected to his attitude to the established religion. After a bad experience, he was worried about a trip to Birmingham:

> I preached in Wednesbury at four, to a nobler people, and was greatly comforted among them; […]

> After preaching again at one, I rode to Birmingham. This had been long a dry, uncomfortable place; so I expected little good here. But I was happily disappointed. Such a congregation I never saw there before: not a scoffer, nor a trifler, not an inattentive person (so far as I could discern) among them; […] Will then God at length cause even this barren wilderness to blossom and bud as the rose?[24]

Alongside the great increase in travel for economic reasons, there was a growth in the number of people travelling for enjoyment – to see the country and sniff some different air. One such pioneer was Thomas Pennant. Compared to Defoe, he shows himself to be

---

[24] Guldi, 2012, and Wesley, 1951.

more interested in the past than the present, but he provides some useful insights. He likes Tamworth, for instance:

> The beauty of the situation of Tamworth is seen from the castle to great advantage, varied with rich meadows, two bridges of the Tame and the Ankor, and the rivers wandering picturesquely along the country.

And he gives some insights into the economy of Coventry:

> The trade of this city consisted originally in the manufacture of cloth and caps or bonnets, [...] and for a long time [the worsted business] proved very extensive and profitable, but this gradually migrated into Leicestershire and Northamptonshire.[25]
>
> About eighty years ago, the silk manufacture of ribands was introduced here, and for the first thirty years, remained in the hands of a few people, who acquired vast fortunes; since when it has extended to a great degree, and is supposed to employ at least ten thousand people; it has likewise spread into the neighbouring towns, such as Nuneaton, and other places. Such real good results from our little vanities!

Pennant also toured Wales, which became a popular destination for travellers from England, and particularly artists. The first major painter of the Snowdonia landscape was Richard Wilson, who was born in mid-Wales and took up landscape painting in Italy in the 1750s before returning to paint his native country. Other artists included Edward Dayes, who painted the English Bridge in Shrewsbury, and produced an engraving of the bridge at Llangollen, as well as pictures of Snowdonia. J M W Turner

---

[25] One example of the worsted industry Pennant gives is 'tammies'. I am grateful to my mother for confirming her hunch that this is short for 'tam-o'shanter'. Defoe had also said that 'the manufacture of tammies is their chief employ, and next to that the weaving of ribbons of the meanest kind, chiefly black'.

himself visited in 1798 and 1799, concentrating particularly on the castles of north Wales.

For most people, travel would still be on foot, or by horse, or maybe in a small cart. But over the century, coach travel became more popular and more widespread. A few people were travelling by coach as early as the mid-sixteenth century, and the first scheduled public coach service began before the Civil War, but the real expansion took place after 1700.

People looking back at the coaching era sometimes give it an air of romance. You can see why – the coachman in his

Figure 22 Coachman in livery, Shrewsbury Museum

livery,[26] the powerful horses yoked together working as a team, the coach speeding along the road leaving others in its wake, the arrival at an inn to a welcoming jug of ale and a hearty plate of lamb chops and potatoes... Perhaps in an attempt to recapture this romance, there was a re-creation in 2012 when twenty-four guests took the Monarch and the Nimrod on a four-day trip from the Manor House Hotel in Meriden to the Lion in Shrewsbury. And there is a whole industry of pictures and prints – I even came across one of The Birmingham Tally-Ho Coach, passing The Crown at Holloway, in a hotel room in a village in the Swiss Alps, where by coincidence I was working on this chapter.

For much of the time, however, coach travel wasn't particularly comfortable, or indeed always safe. Jonathan Swift, who often travelled to and from Ireland for business reasons, had some

Figure 23 Coaching picture of Holloway Road

[26] The example in the picture is from Shrewsbury Museum.

characteristic fun at the expense of his fellow passengers, around 1700:

> When soon, by every hillock, rut, and stone,
> Into each other's face by turns we're thrown.
> *This* grandma scolds, *that* coughs, the captain swears,
> The fair one screams and has a thousand fears; [...]
> Sweet company; Next time I do protest, Sir
> I'd rather walk to Dublin ere I'd ride to Chester.[27]

By the middle of the century, coach travel was more common. In Shrewsbury, for example, regular services began in the 1750s, largely on the initiative of an innkeeper named Robert Lawrence, who kept first the Raven and Bell, and then The Lion inn, which is still going strong on Wyle Cop in the centre of the town. By 1764, the 'Machine' was able to reach London in two days, with an overnight stop in Coventry – about half the time Thomas Pennant took as a schoolboy twenty years earlier.[28] Lawrence succeeded in setting up a service from Holyhead to London in 1780, taking three days, with overnight stops in Castle Bromwich, near Birmingham, and Oswestry. He built up custom by making arrangements with nominated inns along the route. The Castle Bromwich stop was unusual, but has a particular interest for me, since I lived there as a small boy.

By the time Robert Lawrence died in the 1780s, coach travel was well established. A plaque was put up in St Julian's church in memory of Lawrence...

> to whose public spirit and unremitting exertions for upwards of
> 30 years in opening of the great road through Wales [...] the

---

[27] Quoted in Harper, 1902.
[28] Trinder, 1984.

public in general have been greatly indebted and will long have to regret his loss.

Estimates of the scale of the service are inevitably approximate, but the number of London-based services may have risen fourfold between 1773 and 1796.[29] Pennant notes that, as ever, the mode of transport and comfort depended partly on resources and partly on preference:

> Families who travelled in their own carriages, contracted with Benson and Co, and were dragged up in the same number of days, by three sets of able horses.
> The single gentlemen, then a hardy race, equipped in jack-boots and trousers up to their middle, rode post through thick and thin, and, guarded against the mire, defied the frequent stumble and fall; arose and pursued their journey with alacrity.

The next major development was when the mail began to be carried by coach rather than on horseback, and this started with the London to Bristol route from 1784. It was a risky business – the mail coaches had their own armed guards – but they paid no tolls at the turnpike gates. St Albans had its first mail coach in 1785, and in the same year, the Holyhead mail began to be transported by coach, travelling via Northampton and Lutterworth to Tamworth and Lichfield, and then to Chester and along the north Wales coast via St Asaph. Efforts were made to use the more direct route via Llangollen in 1808, though this ran into problems because of the state of the road.[30]

As the need for guards highlights, highwaymen were a threat to travellers throughout the century. Some, however, were authors of their own demise. Harry Simms, known as 'Gentleman Harry',

---

[29] Barker and Gerhold, 1993. The estimate is from work by J A Chartres and G L Turnbull.

[30] Williams, 1977, and see Chapter 7.

committed various hold-ups in the 1740s and was pursued along the Holyhead road. Simms gave his pursuers the slip at the Bull Inn at Dunstable, but then drank too much brandy at the Star at Hockliffe, where he was captured.

He continued his travels along the road, but this time under guard on his way to Tyburn and the gallows!

'Gentleman Harry' may have had quite an audience for his demise. In the 1740s, a lady known as Mother Proctor put up 'pews' for spectators – apprentices from around London would come for the afternoon on the eight hanging days a year.

In spite of the risks, the number of passengers was growing, and the size of coaches also increased, bringing economies. In 1700, there was space for six passengers inside, whereas a century or so later, these six would be accompanied by up to a dozen riding on the outside of the vehicle.

Plenty of competition developed, lasting well into the next century. As well as speed, there were questions of prestige, with the people travelling with the official mail feeling a cut above those taking other services. Thomas de Quincey comments:

> Once I remember being on the box of the Holyhead mail, between Shrewsbury and Oswestry, when a tawdry thing from Birmingham, some *Tallyho* or *Highflier*, all flaunting with green and gold, came up alongside of us. What a contrast to our royal simplicity of form and colour is this plebeian wretch!

Apparently the mail coach easily overtook the Birmingham coach.[31]

On the whole, travellers benefited from the fierce competition between coach services, though this sometimes spilled over into downright reckless behaviour. In the 1830s, the Holyhead Mail tried to pass the Chester Mail by heading down the wrong side of

[31] DeQuincey, 1849 (ed. 2003).

the road near St Albans, leading to a fatal accident, and the jailing of both coachmen.

Multiple efforts were made to speed up journeys. One method was to change whole teams of horses and waggoners, which permitted the service to run through the night – better roads also enabled night running as a safer and more comfortable option.[32] So competition developed as to which inns could turn the service round fastest (perhaps a forerunner of the competition that exists between today's pit crews in Formula One!). In London Colney, you can stand where some of the inns used to be, and imagine the coaches careering up, while the staff stood poised to swing into action to change horses and get them out again. The inns located a little above the river were better placed to see the coaches coming and gain a modest but useful advantage in their ability to supply a new team of horses and refreshments in double-quick time. When the White Lion there was sold in 1807, it was marketed as being 'advantageously situated on the north road'.

Another approach was to cut down refreshment breaks. John Gamble wrote of the crowds in the Britannia Inn in Shrewsbury:

> to a delicate person their clamour might have been annoying, but the annoyance of a mail coach company can never be long; the horn sounds and like ghosts on the crowing of the cock, refreshments scarcely tasted, they must hie away.

Another contemporary, writing in 1833, agreed:

> the rapidity with which our stage coaches now travel has almost driven away all conviviality on the road, for should hunger drive

---

[32] Williams, 1977.

you to dine, you are forced to devour your victuals like a cannibal, and then run like a debtor pursued by bailiffs.[33]

All these changes certainly reduced overall travel times: rather like today, some travellers will have gone for maximum speed, while others went at a more leisurely pace.

Tom Brown's journey from London to Rugby brings out a lot about coach travel in the early Victorian period. Brown has little time for fond farewells to his father when the coach arrives for its 3 a.m. start.

> Up goes Tom, the guard catching his hatbox and holding on with one hand, while with the other he claps the horn to his mouth. Toot, toot, toot! the hostlers let go their heads, the four bays plunge at the collar, and away goes the Tally-ho into the darkness, forty-five seconds from the time they pulled up. Hostler, boots, and the Squire stand looking after them under the Peacock lamp.
>
> 'Sharp work!' says the Squire, and goes in again to his bed, the coach being well out of sight and hearing.[34]

Tom gets very cold travelling on top of the coach, but is rewarded with a magnificent breakfast, without apparently having to hurry too much:

> The table [is] covered with the whitest of cloths and of china, and bearing a pigeon-pie, ham, round of cold boiled beef cut from a mammoth ox, and the great loaf of household bread on a wooden trencher. And here comes in the stout head waiter, puffing under a tray of hot viands – kidneys and a steak, transparent rashers and poached eggs, buttered toast and muffins, coffee and tea, all smoking hot. The table can never hold it all.

[33] Guldi, 2012.
[34] *Tom Brown's Schooldays*, quoted in Hughes, 1857.

In parallel with bigger and more reliable coaches, smaller and more flexible vehicles developed, at least for those who could afford them. Dr Johnson travelled up and down the road between his home town of Lichfield and London by coach, once apparently heading south on the same vehicle as the actor David Garrick, in 1737. For pleasure, however, Johnson enthused about the smaller post-chaise, commenting:

> If I had no duties and no reference to futurity, I would spend my life in driving briskly with a pretty woman.[35]

His neighbour, Erasmus Darwin, wasn't so happy, perhaps because he was travelling on more minor roads and on duty as a doctor, rather than for pleasure:

> I, imprisoned in a post chaise, am joggled, and jostled, and bumped, and bruised along the King's high road, to make war upon a pox or a fever![36]

Innkeepers such as Robert Lawrence in Shrewsbury fostered the coaching service because it provided them with plenty of opportunities for expansion. In many cases, coaches were operated by partnerships of innkeepers, who came to dominate the industry. They organised the teams of horses, and the profits were shared out between partners according to the work carried out by their horses. As well as delivering quick turnaround times, success depended on getting the right horses and keeping the costs of the fodder down.

In the heyday of the road, the inns won high praise from some travellers. Baron D'Haussez, a French visitor, wrote:

> Among the wonders of English civilisation, the inns should be mentioned. In many of the larger towns, they are magnificent

[35] Lichfield Museum.
[36] Quoted in Upton, 1993.

and they are good and well supplied in the smallest. In the greater part of them, the servants are in livery, and in all their attendance are prompt and respectful.[37]

Many of the inns which served the coaching trade are still in place today, such as the Hand Hotel, where we stayed in Llangollen. An earlier traveller, the German Prince Puckler-Muskau, made a note of what he had for breakfast there:

> ...steaming coffee, fresh guinea fowl eggs, dark yellow mountain butter, thick cream, toasted muffins and finally two freshly caught trout with delicate red spots.[38]

Not all of those items are on the menu today, but the coffee and the bacon and eggs are still good.

The Irish politician, Daniel O'Connell, preferred the King's Head in the same town, writing in its visitors' book:

> I remember this village with very bad cheer
> Ere the Ladies, God bless them, set this inn here;
> But the traveller now is sure of good fare,
> Let him stay at this inn, or go to that 'ere;
> But all who can read will sure understand
> How vastly superior's the Head to the Hand.[39]

The Ladies in question were Eleanor Butler and Sarah Ponsonby, who left Ireland in the 1770s since – most unusually for those days – they chose each other's company rather than marriage, and set up home at Plas Newydd, near Llangollen. This quickly attracted attention in high places, and the ladies' visitors included William Wordsworth, Robert Browning, Sir Walter Scott, and Alfred Lord Tennyson, along with the Duke of Wellington, all of whom are said to have stayed at the Hand.

---

[37] Quoted in Quartermaine, 2006, written in 1833.
[38] Quoted in Quartermaine, 2006, written in 1828.
[39] Quoted in Harper, 1902.

The hotel also developed a reputation for music. The late nineteenth-century diarist, Francis Kilvert, commented:

> As we came near the Hand, we heard the strains of the Welsh harp, the first I've ever heard. The harper [sic] was playing in the hall, the air 'Jenny Jones'. I had come all the way to Llangollen on purpose to hear the Welsh harp: this is the only hotel in Wales where the Welsh harp can be heard.

The musical tradition continues: the hotel provides rehearsal space for a male voice choir, who were performing in the bar after their rehearsal on a Friday evening during our stay.[40]

Another surviving coaching house in Llangollen is the Wynnstay Arms, which has an example of a common twentieth-century modification – the big gateway which used to lead to the stables often leads to the car park today. The inn was probably built in the seventeenth century, and until the mid-nineteenth century was known as the Eagles Inn, after the spread eagle still visible on the sign, which comes from the coat of arms of the polysyllabic Sir Watkin Williams Wynn, who owned the land. The inn retains the mounting block at the main entrance to help travellers on and off their horses.

Competition among inns prompted publicans to look for new ways to set themselves apart from their rivals. Pennant refers to an example in Hockley in the Hole (Hockliffe), 'a long range of houses, mostly inns', where:

> The English rage of novelty is strongly tempted by one sagacious publican, who informs us on his sign, of newspapers being to be seen at his house every day in the week.[41]

---

[40] Information from visit there in June 2014.
[41] Pennant, 1811.

Figure 24 Wynnstay Arms, Llangollen, showing mounting block

Others went in for concerts, games of skittles or quoits, and billiards.[42] Some inns were big business: the Dun Cow at Dunchurch could house 120 pairs of horses.

A number of towns became heavily dependent on travellers. Defoe describes Daventry as:

> A considerable market town, but which subsists chiefly by the great concourse of travellers on the old Watling Street way, which lies near it.

Pennant notes that Dunstable – 'a long town, built on each side of the Watling Street' – is 'supported chiefly by the great passage of travellers. A small neat manufacture of straw-hats, and baskets, and

---

[42] Guldi, 2012.

toys, maintains many of the poor'. Its population roughly doubled between 1760 and 1801.[43]

London Colney, the other side of St Albans, had twenty-six inns in the village at one point, typically working in pairs, with one looking after the gentry and the other taking care of the servants and coachmen.[44] The inns may have provided employment, but not everyone welcomed the passing trade. In 1823, a local vicar said:

> London Colney being on the high London road, and full of public houses, exposes its people to examples and temptations, which must necessarily cause the Sabbath to be lamentably neglected, or spent in an indecent and disorderly manner.[45]

Greater prosperity and stability was reflected in the building and development of a number of stately homes along the route. Defoe describes Cannons in Edgware (now known as Canons Park) as 'a most magnificent palace or mansion house, I might say, the most magnificent in England'.[46] As well as building a fine house, the owner, the Duke of Chandos, filled it with works of art, and also music – he employed George Frederick Handel as his composer in residence, and he wrote his 'Chandos Anthems' there.

The house was replaced by a smaller one in the mid-1700s, which is now part of the North London Collegiate School, and the grounds are an attractive public park. The gateposts still stand, fronting on to Watling Street, maybe fifteen feet high, each topped with a monumental urn. They must have made a powerful statement, both to guests at Chandos, and to the local people

---

[43] Pawson, 1977.
[44] London Colney Local History Society, *The Record*, spring 2014.
[45] Ibid.
[46] Defoe, Letter 6.

outside, who only ever passed by rather than through on their business along the road.

Further north is Weston Park, just on the Staffordshire side of the border with Shropshire. Travellers along the road in the 1760s would have seen a lot of work taking place on the remodelling of the seventeenth-century house into a grander mansion. The owner, Sir Henry Bridgeman (later Baron Bradford), commissioned Capability Brown, the leading landscape gardener of the day, to lay out the park, which incorporates a medieval deer park. The house was gifted to the nation in 1986. It is now used for business events and is available for hire for weddings or other celebrations. It's also used as one of the venues for the V Festival, so in 2015 – unless they arrived by helicopter – the A5 played host to Justin Timberlake, Ed Sheeran, the Manic Street Preachers and (more my generation) Blondie, who entertained some 90 000 visitors.

Figure 25 Gates of Canons Park, Edgware

A few miles further west, in Atcham just outside Shrewsbury, is Attingham Park, built by the Hill family between 1782 and 1785 – Noel Hill became Lord Berwick, after being MP for Shrewsbury from 1768. Journeys were disrupted soon after that as Berwick made more room for himself by moving the Holyhead road further from the house, though the building is still clearly visible from the road through Atcham. Its fortunes waxed and waned over the years as different members of the family took charge, not all choosing to live there.

The house is open to the public, thanks to the National Trust, and offers some fascinating insights into eighteenth-century life. At each place on the large table in the servants' hall is a plate, not now for eating from, but to give details such as the name, job title, and duties of the member of staff who would have sat there in the late eighteenth century. Responsibility for travel was clearly important: the head coachman, Frederick Nash, was the highest-ranking servant wearing livery, and paid 35 guineas a year, or £5,800 in today's money.[47] One of the footmen, Henry Faulkus, was responsible for carriage duties, and kept a disbursement book to account for all expenditure, including tollgate fees, as well as gifts to the poor from Lady Berwick. He was paid 28 guineas a year for these responsibilities. Villagers are still able to walk their dogs in the park, and I went for a run there while staying at the pub for a night.

Other areas became more built up in denser and less scenic ways. Miners' cottages became more prevalent around the coalfields of South Staffordshire. The turnpiking of a stretch of road in Birmingham led to development in Deritend, according to Hutton:

---

[47] A guinea was a pound and an old shilling, so £1.05. The comparison to today comes from the Bank of England inflation calculator.

It does not appear that Deritend was attended with any considerable augmentation from the Norman conquest to the year 1767, when a turnpike road was opened to Alcester, and when Henry Bradford publicly offered a freehold to the man who should first build upon his estate; since which time Deritend has made a rapid progress, and this dusky offspring of Birmingham is now travelling apace along her new formed road.[48]

The eighteenth century saw greater prosperity and peace, at least at home. More people travelled, for a greater range of reasons, and by different methods. The turnpike system improved the management of the road, but the struggle between upkeep and demand remained a struggle. William Hutton, writing towards the end of the century, noted differences between the roads around Birmingham:

> Upon the Lichfield road, to the disgrace of the community, is yet a river without a bridge. […]The road to Wolverhampton is much improved since the coal-teams left it. The road to Dudley is despicable beyond description. That to Coventry can only be equalled by the Dudley road. The genius of the age has forgot, in some of these roads to accommodate the foot passenger with a causeway.

As the century approached its end, the route to Holyhead was one of several main roads which were not serving travellers well. Events the far side of the Irish Sea meant that the history of our road over the next few years was to be very different from the others.

---

[48] Hutton, 1783. The Henry Bradford referred to is probably the same man as Sir Henry Bridgeman from Weston Park, though he did not become Baron Bradford until 1794.

Chapter 7

Telford and the Improvement of the Road, 1810–1835

Good roads, canals, and navigable rivers, by diminishing the expense of carriage, put the remotest parts of a country nearly on a level with those in the neighbourhood of a town; they are, upon that account, the greatest of all improvements.

—Adam Smith[1]

By the start of the nineteenth century, the Holyhead road was under strain. This problem applied to many major roads in the kingdom. The solution was unique.

In 1800, following a period of turbulent relations leading to a rebellion, the Westminster Parliament passed the Act of Union with Ireland, which abolished the Irish Parliament and brought the government of the two kingdoms together. Holyhead was the main port for journeys to and from Dublin. Irish MPs and peers sat in the London Parliament, and officials and others had to travel to Ireland more often, as London took a more hands-on role in the government of the Emerald Isle. And it was ever more important

[1] Quoted in Parnell, 1833.

117

to get the mail to and fro safely, reliably and quickly. So pressure on the road grew rapidly, and the problems which were emerging before 1800 came centre stage. Nor were they confined to the physical state of the road: the archaeologist and traveller, Sir Richard Colt Hoare, much disliked travel through Wales, where he found 'People (like the country) rude and uncivilised: roads infested by herds of beggars and children turned to begging by incessantly following the carriage for great distances'.[2]

As with infrastructure projects today, however, it was some time before comprehensive action was taken. Lobbying from Irish MPs led to improvements in the harbours at Holyhead and Howth, near Dublin, and money was provided in 1807 for this purpose.[3] But that was of limited value given the poor quality of the roads either side. According to a Parliamentary report, the Holyhead road was 'in bad repair, in many places dangerous, in almost all too narrow, frequently ascending hills unnecessarily, and following lines incapable of improvement'.[4] An attempt by the Post Office to extend the mail coach service to Holyhead ran into trouble when, at one point, three post horses fell and broke their legs within a single week. A later report talked of the need to be able to travel through Wales 'without being exposed to be broken in pieces at every step, or to the danger of falling over steep precipices, against which the road was not in the smallest degree protected'.[5] The road across Anglesey, for example, was described as 'A miserable tract, composed of a succession of circuitous and craggy inequalities'.[6]

By March 1810, Parliament decided to get moving – or at least to get talking. The House of Commons appointed a committee

[2] Diary, 1806, quoted in Quartermaine, 2003.
[3] Rolt, 1958.
[4] Quoted in Hughes, 1964.
[5] Quoted in Select Committee Second Report.
[6] Rolt, 1958.

to look into the roads to Holyhead, from Chester as well as from Shrewsbury, and to assess 'what improvements may be practicable therein for the convenience of travellers'.[7] The case for action had already been made – the Committee noted:

> the Postmasters General made a representation in the year 1808 to the Lords Commissioners of the Treasury, of the bad and dangerous state of this road [...] concluding 'And my Lords confidently hope that the public spirit of the gentlemen of the country, their regard for the lives of travellers, and their consideration of the value of the new Mail Coach, [...] will induce them immediately to take means for effecting the necessary repairs and improvements.[8]

These representations had proved 'ineffectual'. As a result 'several very serious accidents happened [and] in a space of 85 days ending the 27th March 1810, the mail coach was late in its arrival at Holyhead 71 times, from one to five hours, and on its arrival at Shrewsbury 75 times'.[9]

To start to get a grip on the issue, Thomas Telford was appointed to conduct a survey of the problem and identify possible solutions.

Telford was then in his early fifties. The only child of a Scottish shepherd from the Borders, he had begun his working life as a stonemason. He knew sections of the Holyhead road from being the first Surveyor of Public Works for the County of Salop (Shropshire), a post which he held from 1787 to the day he died in 1834. He was a man of immense energy. Around the turn of the century, he was dividing his time between three major ventures. Most men would have found enough to do in the building of the Ellesmere

---

[7] Quoted in Hughes, 1964.
[8] Quoted in Select Committee Second Report.
[9] Ibid.

Canal, including the innovative Pontcysyllte Aqueduct, soaring 126 feet above the Vale of Llangollen, and still well worth a visit. But at the same time, Telford was delivering major improvements to the roads in Scotland, particularly in the Highlands, and also making a reality of the oft-mooted idea of a canal from Fort William to Inverness. Perhaps Parliament worked on the principle that the best way to get something done was to ask a busy person.

Telford's initial role was to produce a survey and report on where an improved road might go. As a later committee commented:

> Mr Telford was able to lay before the Lords of the Treasury a Plan
> by which the distance would be shortened four miles between
> Shrewsbury and Holyhead, and by which all the inclinations of
> the hills would be reduced by one foot in thirty.[10]

The MPs made their report in May 1811, and were persuaded of the scale of the problem. But at much the same time, once one of the key supporters of upgrading the road, John Foster retired to the House of Lords when his post of Chancellor of the Irish Exchequer was abolished, so real action did not follow until 1815 – as a future report put it, 'except in only a very few places, this road remained in the same dangerous and imperfect state up to the Session of 1815'.[11]

It was only when Sir Henry Parnell, MP for Queen's County in Ireland, became involved that the plan moved from concept to reality. He established a new Parliamentary committee with himself as chairman. In their first report, they strengthened the case for action. As well as the mail traffic, trade was growing, then 'exceeding twenty millions in annual value'. Union with England meant that appeals from the Irish courts now went to the English

[10] Ibid.
[11] Ibid.

courts. Family connections were strong, and the 'better classes' in Ireland educated their children in England.[12]

Others had identified the need for action: Parnell's key achievement was also to deliver the funding. In June 1815, he persuaded the House of Commons Committee of Supply to make available £20,000 for the repair of the Holyhead road, and the necessary Bill received Royal Assent on 11 July 1815.

It's hard to appreciate, from today's vantage point, how radical a step this was. Since the end of the First World War, we have looked mostly to government to build the nation's infrastructure, but that was not the approach in previous centuries. Road improvements in 1815 were in the hands of the turnpike trusts. The canals had been built with private money. The same approach was to apply to the railways in the 1830s – the private investment under the Private Finance Initiative of the 1990s was in some ways a return to previous approaches. Certainly, in 1815, it was public finance which was the radical new step. The call had come from MPs in 1811, who advised that 'without considerable aid from the public to the funds of those Roads [...] no real permanent assistance can be given to support the intercourse between Great Britain and Ireland by Holyhead'.[13] It was Parnell who turned that into cash.

In contrast to today's lengthy mobilisation periods, work on the Holyhead road began swiftly once the funding was agreed. A Commission was set up under Parnell's leadership, including the future prime minister, Robert Peel (then Chief Secretary for Ireland), William Huskisson (First Commissioner of Woods, Forests and Land Revenues) and Charles Watkin Williams Wynn. They met for the first time within a fortnight of the legislation passing, and appointed Alexander Milne as Secretary, and Telford as

[12] Hughes, 1964.
[13] Quoted in Select Committee Second Report.

Engineer. On the basis of 'worst first', they decided to start with the section from Shrewsbury to Bangor Ferry – Telford described the latter section of that, from Cernioge, as '28 miles of the most difficult and dangerous part of the Holyhead Road'.[14] The work itself got under way in October 1815.

Alongside supervising the rebuilding of these sections, Telford spent the first eighteen months on a detailed survey of the whole route. He identified 28 relatively small-scale improvements to sections of road, ranging in length from 270 yards in Towcester to over three miles between Barnet and South Mimms.[15] The works in England started with the Archway Road in Highgate only three miles from the centre of London, and ended with a section at Chirk Bridge on the Welsh border. Telford's final report notes, for example, that 'An extensive improvement has been made at Hockliffe Hills' – not surprising given the problems recounted by Celia Fiennes a century earlier, which had clearly not been solved, in spite of Defoe's enthusiasm. The Select Committee, reviewing progress in 1830, also noted positive comments from coach owners about the work on the Archway Road.[16]

In Wales, Telford effectively rebuilt the whole road, and his work forms the basis for the A5 through Snowdonia today, commemorated with brown signs showing a coach.

All this effort and investment had the desired effect: Parnell wrote that before the improvements the Holyhead road 'between London and Birmingham was one of the worst roads in England. The consequence was that nearly all the travelling [...]

[14] Ibid.

[15] This precision comes from Appendix IV of Parnell, 1833, which gives the whole of the Report of the Select Committee appointed to look into the spending on the improvement of the Holyhead and Liverpool roads, which reported on 30 May 1830.

[16] Quoted in Parnell, 1833.

Figure 26 Brown sign, in Wales, marking the coaching road

was by Oxford, though the longest road by eight miles; but now the travelling has been transferred to the Coventry line'.[17]

One of the reasons for Telford's success was to combine energy with a passion for quality and attention to detail. This started with the foundations of the roads. In his third Annual Report to Parliament, he comments:

> I cannot too often repeat, that a surveyor should not feel satisfied that he has done his duty until the whole breadth of the ground belonging to a road […] is put into perfect order, as this shows skill, attention, and good workmanship.[18]

He paid a lot of attention to straightening the road and reducing gradients, so that, for example, the climb into the Snowdonia mountains up Nant Ffrancon, from Bethesda to the highest point

[17] Parnell, 1833.
[18] Quoted in Parnell, 1833.

on the road, is less than 1 in 20, compared to 1 in 6 on the previous road.

Telford's precision extended to the features which made a road function. He provided a detailed specification for toll houses, which 'should be built in a strong and substantial manner, and made suitable and comfortable for the persons who are to inhabit them'. His concern for the occupants extends to quite personal matters: 'In this garden, a privy is to be built, with proper roof, dome, seat, etc complete'.

Toll houses on the mainland were single-storey, and there is a good example still standing near Glyndyfrdwy, just west of Llangollen. Toll houses on Anglesey, however, had two storeys with an octagonal tower, and the best surviving example on the whole road stands in Llanfair PG, with the tolls clearly visible, though the privy in the garden isn't around any longer. We were told, by the way, that the toll board from Glydyfrdwy was taken

Figure 27 Toll house near Llangollen

Figure 28 Toll house in Llanfair PG

Figure 29 Toll board in Llanfair PG

to the village hall for safekeeping some time ago, and that the powers-that-be had refused to return it – a local version of the Elgin Marbles?

Similarly, the location and design of tollgates was specified in great detail. 'Many fatal accidents have occurred from having toll-gates just at the bottom of hills. [...] Toll-gates should be painted white, to make them more easily seen in the night time.'[19]

Figure 30 Sunburst gate, Anglesey

Finally, travellers could track their progress by the uniform design of milestones, many of which are still by the roadside, such as this one a few miles into Anglesey from the Menai Bridge.[20] Again, there was a standard design, intended to be read out of the

---

[19] Ibid.
[20] Quartermaine, 2003, says that only five out of the original eighty-three are missing.

Figure 31 Milestone, Anglesey

window of a moving carriage, and to give passengers the distance both to Holyhead itself and to the next inn, as well as from the last major staging post.[21]

Not surprisingly, Telford's attention to detail led to annoyance when impertinent locals didn't go along with what he wanted. In Allesley, on the outskirts of Coventry, he lowered the road to make the gradient more manageable, and put in new driveways for the residents, only to find that 'the parish have erected on the road-side a very ugly rude pump, and have left the surface of the ground round it in a very slovenly state'.[22]

---

[21] Ibid.

[22] Telford's report to Parliament, quoted in an April 2014 article by Chris Upton on the *Birmingham Post* website.

Having rebuilt the road, Telford and Parnell wanted to ensure that it was better managed for the long term, so that the improvements would stick. They persuaded Parliament to pass an Act in May 1819 to put one turnpike trust in charge of the 100 miles or so of road on the mainland west of Shrewsbury, in place of the seven which had previously shared the job. They reformed the structure of the trust: it had only fifteen commissioners, which may sound a lot, but there were no fewer than 300 for the previous Oswestry trust alone.[23] The trust was also required to appoint a professional surveyor to lead its work, and to report direct to Parliament on progress.

Another Act of 1819 provided for the construction of a completely new road across Anglesey, with a new bridge across the Menai Straits to reach the island. This was also much-needed. The Straits had been crossed down the centuries by various means – Suetonius used a mix of barges and getting his horses to swim, whereas Edward I fashioned impromptu wooden bridges from boats and planks. By the seventeenth century, ferry crossings were established, but the currents were tricky and there was a history of boats running aground or capsizing.

To carry the traffic, Telford designed and built the first modern suspension bridge in the world. As well as contending with the geography, he had to ensure that the bridge was high enough for Royal Navy ships up to 100 feet high to pass underneath, not only once it was complete, but through the construction period too – the Napoleonic Wars were fresh in the memory. The towers at either end are made of limestone from Penmon on Anglesey itself, which was also used for the nearby Britannia Bridge, built by Robert Stephenson thirty years later for rail traffic, and for Birmingham Town Hall, 150 miles or so back down the Holyhead road. Across the 176 metres (577 feet) in

Figure 32 The Menai Bridge

between the towers, the builders erected sixteen chain cables each weighing over 120 tons.

The bridge opened on 30 January 1826. The *Chester Chronicle* commented:

> Tickets could not be issued fast enough for the demand [...] The evening was spent by the workmen with much fun and feasting, [...] wishing "Success to the bridge"[24]

Stagecoaches paid a toll of 2 shillings and sixpence – over £10 in today's money[25] –with different tariffs for different vehicles, and a penny for people wanting to walk across.

There was one more problem to crack. To complete the journey to Holyhead, passengers had to get across the Stanley Sands. Telford

---

[24] Quoted in Williams, 1977.
[25] Based on the Bank of England inflation calculator.

built a new embankment running for well over half a mile, requiring, he noted with characteristic precision, 156,271 cubic yards of earth and 25,754 cubic yards of rubble stone. His report concluded in a way perhaps intended to be literal, rather than conceited: 'It has been completed seven years and is now in a perfect state'.[26]

Holyhead itself shared in the development. The packet station at the port was built in about 1809, with a notable clock added in the 1820s. That decade also saw the pier built, though the lighthouse at the end was only used for a couple of years. The arch marking the end of the road was built properly in stone in 1823 – a wooden arch had been put up hastily when George IV passed through the port earlier, but was replaced by the more robust structure which still stands today.

Figure 33 Holyhead: an early port administration building

[26] Telford's report to the Select Committee appointed to look into the spending on the improvement of the Holyhead and Liverpool roads, which reported on 30 May 1830, quoted in Parnell, 1833.

Figure 34 The Holyhead arch

The total spent on Telford's works was nearly £700,000. It's clearly very hard to make meaningful comparisons. The best estimates of changes in the general price level suggest this would be equivalent to nearly £60 billion today, which dwarfs the cost of the M25 at about £2.5 billion, and exceeds the projected cost of the High Speed 2 railway, including rolling stock, at around £50 billion.[27] So Telford had plenty of money, but not quite a blank cheque. There were some disputes with the Treasury – which sound familiar to me as a former Treasury official! – when the cost of the iron for the Menai Bridge rose, and 'the Commissioners felt themselves justified […] in representing to the Treasury

[27] The Bank of England website has an inflation calculator, used throughout, which compares price levels back to 1750, and up to 2012. This generates a very precise figure as the equivalent of £700,000 in 1820: £57,292,307.69!

that the difference [...] exceeded £4,500, but this claim was not admitted'.[28]

Overall, the Parliamentary committee – no doubt reflecting Parnell's own satisfaction with the project – noted:

> As it appears that several of the contractors have failed, the Committee consider this as a proof that the prices [...] could not have been beyond what were fair and sufficient.

History is written by the victors,[29] and Telford and Parnell were clearly skilled at their own propaganda.[30] Telford, as an engineer, had a number of things going for him: there was a clear case for improving the road; a political ally in Parnell; and plenty of public money, regularly topped up, to support a road-building technique which was high-quality but expensive compared to his contemporary John McAdam, for instance.[31] But the benefits were clear. An independent witness, William Waterhouse, a coach master, told a different group of MPs in 1819 that the new roads in north Wales were 'in the best form I have ever seen roads made.' He expanded:

> They are laid in a form sufficiently round to wash themselves, if there is a shower of rain [...] They are not very high; and their excellence consists in the smallness of the convexity.

---

[28] Report of 1830, quoted in Parnell, 1833. This sort of discussion is certainly familiar to me, having worked on public spending in the Treasury from 1996 to 1999, and from 2009 to 2011.

[29] Often attributed to Sir Winston Churchill, but nobody seems absolutely sure.

[30] There is a whole book by Charles Hadfield, *Thomas Telford's Temptation*, which is mostly about his work on canals, which argues that Telford sought to do down the reputation of another leading engineer, William Jessop, in a number of ways, so that Telford himself would be regarded as the undisputed master of iron canal aqueducts, and the man responsible for the Ellesmere and Caledonian canals.

[31] Hindle, 1993.

Another regular traveller, C T S Birch Reynardson, commented that:

> The road was so good, that unless you went to a stone-heap, I don't think you could have found a stone big enough to pelt a robin with.[32]

Mail delivery times between London and Holyhead fell from 38 hours in 1808 to less than 27 hours in 1836, with 27 changes of horses. The specified timings involved leaving London at 8 p.m., changing horses at Towcester (among other places) at 2 o'clock in the morning, reaching Birmingham just after 7 a.m. for breakfast, Shrewsbury at midday, Capel Curig at 7 o'clock in the evening, and Holyhead in time for a nightcap just before 11 p.m. One service, the Independent Tally-Ho, covered the 109 miles from Birmingham to London in 7 hours and 39 minutes in May 1830, an achievement described as 'unparalleled in the annals of coaching' by the *Coventry Chronicle*.[33]

Traffic increased, sometimes dramatically: a report to Parliament noted a doubling of the number of carriages, chaises, and gigs crossing through the tollgates on a section of the Holyhead Road between 1824 and 1828.[34] Seventy-two coaches a day were running through St Albans at the peak.[35] Comfort, safety and reliability all improved. The works enabled people to take a range of journeys which would previously have been impossible or barely worth the effort: more merchants did business with Ireland; Irish people started going to spas in Malvern or Bath; and more tourists were able to enjoy the natural beauties of north Wales.[36] More practically, the Parliamentary committee could point to cash savings from

[32] Quoted in Williams, 1977.

[33] Williams, 1977.

[34] Comparative Statement of the Travelling, through one of the gates in the Commissioners' Hands 1, Commissioners of Shrewsbury and Holyhead roads, Report 1828 (168), 4., referrred to in Guldi, 2012.

[35] St Albans museum.

[36] This breakdown appears in Quartermaine, 2003.

abolishing the separate revenue boards for Britain and Ireland, and transferring the management of Ireland's revenues to London.[37]

One of those to benefit was Charles Dickens, who made a number of journeys along the Holyhead road. He stayed at the Cock Inn in Stony Stratford more than once, and a nice teashop nearby is named Miss Havisham's in tribute. He also stayed at the Lion Hotel in Shrewsbury, and gave readings at the Music Hall, which is now the excellent town museum. In December 1853, 2,000 people waited outside Birmingham Town Hall in the snow for a reading of *A Christmas Carol* by Dickens.

One of Dickens's most famous creations, Samuel Pickwick, journeyed back to London by coach from an expedition to the Midlands. He stayed at the Royal Hotel in Birmingham (long since gone), and then headed for home. He had bad luck with the weather, but ploughed on:

> Although the roads were miry, [...] and although the mud and wet splashed in at the open windows of the carriage [...] still there was something in the very motion [...] which was so infinitely superior to being pent in a dull room.[38]

They first changed horses at Coventry, 'where the steam ascended from the horses in such clouds as wholly to obscure the hostler'. They stopped at Dunchurch and Daventry, and 'at the end of each stage it rained harder than it had done at the beginning'. The party decided to stay the night at the Saracens Head in Towcester, on the recommendation of Samuel Weller:

> everything clean, and comfortable. Wery good little dinner, Sir, they can get ready in half an hour – pair of fowls, Sir, and a weal cutlet; French beans, 'taturs, tart, and tidiness.

---

[37] Report of 1830 quoted in Parnell, 1833.
[38] Dickens, *The Pickwick Papers*.

Figure 35 Towcester, The Saracens Head

The dinner menu has changed somewhat, but the Saracens Head is still thriving, and I have enjoyed the breakfast there myself.

Telford died in 1834. The road was at its zenith in importance, and turnpike rights were sought after. In Lichfield Museum, there is a notice of an 1830 auction of the rights to the tolls, posted by the Clerk to the Trustees, Thomas Hinckley. These rights ran for a year, and the first district, for instance, running from Coleshill to Stone via Lichfield, including the Curdworth gate and sidebar, had a reserve price of £270 – £27,500 in today's money.[39]

A few years later, the price would have dropped considerably. The road's period of popularity was far shorter than anyone could have expected when the improvements were commissioned in 1815. The railways saw to that.

[39] Bank of England inflation calculator.

Chapter 8

Railways, Industry, and Politicians: The Road in the Nineteenth Century

> *Five and thirty years ago, the glory had not yet departed from the old coach roads: the great roadside inns were still brilliant with well-polished tankards, the smiling glances of pretty barmaids, and the repartees of jocose ostlers; the mail still announced itself by the merry notes of the horn; the hedge-cutter or the rick-thatcher might still know the exact hour by the unfailing yet otherwise meteoric apparition of the pea-green Tally-ho or the yellow Independent.*
>
> — *Felix Holt: The Radical*, George Eliot, 1866

On 23 December 1837, the railway engineer, George Stephenson, had dinner with his son Robert and some colleagues at the Dun Cow inn, in Dunchurch in Warwickshire, to celebrate the completion of the Kilsby Tunnel, another step towards the completion of the Birmingham to London railway. It was understandable that they should want to celebrate. The tunnel had caused a lot of trouble: a collapsing roof and flooding meant the cost was three times the original estimate, and the opening of the railway as a whole was delayed as a result.

The venue for the celebration was a well-established coaching inn on the Holyhead road. While the proprietors were no doubt glad of Stephenson's business at the time, they may not have guessed at the impact which the onward march of the railways would have for the road, and hence for the inns and indeed villages along the way.

There had actually been interest in bringing steam-driven transport to the roads: a vehicle designed by W G and R Heaton, from Birmingham, went up and down the road to Wolverhampton twice in a day in 1833, with thirty people on board, and then went the other way along the Holyhead road to Coventry and back. But its backers found the 'results of experiments not satisfactory', according to one source, and it was another sixty years before a viable form of mechanical road transport was discovered.[1]

Instead, the railways spread rapidly. The Grand Junction railway opened in July 1837, linking Birmingham to the Liverpool and Manchester Railway, via Wolverhampton and Crewe. In April 1838, a few months after the Dunchurch celebration, the first train from Euston station in London came through to a place called Denbigh Hall, in what's now Milton Keynes. Denbigh Hall had been used as a camp to house the workers building the line, since it was the point where the tracks crossed Watling Street. For a few months, it was the end of the line, and stagecoaches took passengers on to Rugby, where they could pick up the train again, until the full London to Birmingham route was opened in September 1838, taking in Rugby and Coventry, as it still does today.

Denbigh Hall was only ever a temporary measure, but a very long-lasting facility opened nearby as early as 1838 in the form of the Wolverton railway works, roughly halfway along the new line from London to Birmingham. Wolverton itself was created as a Victorian new town on the back of this, and Stony Stratford found that the loss of business on Watling Street was offset by its involvement in the railway works, which was joined by a tramway. Wolverton continued to make trains in quantity until after the Beeching cuts of the 1960s, including many carriages for successive Royal trains.

[1] Upton, 1993, and *Grace's Guide to British Industrial History* at www.graces-guide.co.uk.

The rail link to Liverpool soon took traffic away from the Holyhead road. Combining the two railways and the fast steam packet ships from Liverpool to Dun Laoghaire (then known as Kingstown), the journey time from London to Dublin was 22½ hours, compared to 30 hours by road, even after Telford's improvements. So from 24 January 1839, the Irish Mail went by rail. The route via north Wales remained shorter, of course, so strenuous efforts were made to build a railway line to Holyhead. This was completed in 1850, with Robert Stephenson again heavily involved.

Nearly all the other main towns along the road were also connected by 1860. Bletchley station was built in 1847, a mile or so off the road, and Fenny Stratford station had opened a year earlier, carrying the line to Bedford – that station is very close to Watling Street, and the carriageway had to be raised by more than six feet to go over the line. The station in Shrewsbury opened in 1848, to operate a line to Chester, and the link to Birmingham was established in 1854. St Albans was connected in 1858 by a branch line from Watford. The Vale of Llangollen Railway opened to freight on 1 December 1861, and to passengers on 2 June 1862. It reached Corwen in May 1865.

The impact of the railways on the road was very quick. Toll income for the eight trusts between London and Birmingham more or less halved straight after the railway opened.[2] Initially the coach services tried to compete – in the spring of 1838, the well-known Shrewsbury-based coach, the Wonder, left Euston at the same time as the Birmingham train, and reached its destination twenty minutes earlier.[3] But the advantage couldn't last. Not long after that, a resident of Shrewsbury wrote:

> Shrewsbury seems to be a declining town. […] The Manchester and Liverpool railway to Birmingham has had a very great and disadvantageous effect upon this town, which has almost ceased

[2] Barker and Savage, 1974.
[3] Dyos and Aldcroft, 1971.

to be a thoroughfare and it was a great one; consequently many of the coaches have been given up. We are getting quite insulated.[4]

The following year, Henry Gray, a postmaster from Birmingham, told a Parliamentary committee that the loss of horse-drawn coaches had been 'very great'.

The special approach given to the Holyhead road came to an end. By 1851, with the rail link complete, the Commissioners made their twenty-eighth and final report to the Parliamentary Select Committee, with perhaps an air of sadness:

> We are of the opinion that the road is no longer of such national importance as to justify us in applying to Parliament for a grant of public money for its future maintenance.[5]

The turnpike trusts waned in importance. They prompted controversy in some quarters for their impact on the poor. The writer and rural champion William Cobbett had commented in 1830 that 'the turnpike toll for the poor man's ass is the same as for the hunter or the racer or carriage horse of the lord', and a few years later popular discontent over tolls helped prompt the Rebecca Riots in Wales, which spread briefly to north London.[6] A Parliamentary select committee suggested abolishing turnpikes in 1864, and they gradually fell away, with the last one disappearing in 1885.

The approach to road management changed. Before the advent of the railways, the General Highway Act of 1835 abolished regulations on loads and wheel design, and gave responsibility for roads to local vestries, but since there were around 15,000 of these, they proved too small to do the job. Parliament returned to the issue in the 1862 Highways Act, which sought to strengthen highways authorities, but even by 1880, there were still over 400 highway districts and 6,000

[4] Quoted in Trinder, 1984.
[5] Quoted in Quartermaine et al., 2003.
[6] *Two-penny trash, or Politics for the Poor*, quoted in Guldi, 2012.

parishes looking after their own roads. Only in 1888, when the Local Government Act gave the new county councils responsibility for all main roads, was there a more streamlined system.[7]

Charles Dickens gives a vivid sketch of the impact of the railways on the coaching trade, no doubt with a bit of artistic licence, in one of the chapters of *The Uncommercial Traveller*. 'An Old Stage-Coaching House' first appeared in 1863.[8] It's not clear where the traveller was writing about, and experts believe it was on the Great West Road rather than the Holyhead road, but the position is likely to be similar. Dickens first visits the inn:

> The old room on the ground floor, where the passengers of the Highflyer used to dine, had nothing in it but a wretched show of twigs and flower-pots in the broad window to hide the nakedness of the land [...] The other room, where post-horse company used to wait while relays were getting ready down the yard, still held its ground, but was as airless as I conceive a hearse to be.

The condition of the turnpike gates themselves was no better.

> The Turnpike-house was all overgrown with ivy; and the Turnpike-keeper, unable to get a living out of the tolls, plied the trade of a cobbler. Not only that, but his wife sold ginger-beer, and, in the very window of espial through which the Toll-takers of old times used with awe to behold the grand London coaches coming on at a gallop, exhibited for sale little barber's-poles of sweetstuff in a sticky lantern.
> The political economy of the master of the turnpike thus expressed itself.

---

[7] Dyos and Aldcroft, 1971.
[8] Dickens, 1863.

"How goes turnpike business, master?" said I to him, as he sat in his little porch, repairing a shoe.

"It don't go at all, master," said he to me. "It's stopped."

The advent of the railways did not mean that roads were no longer needed – rather, it changed the nature of the journeys undertaken. Shorter trips to and from stations replaced the long-haul coach journeys. MPs noted in 1839 that 'nearly all roads or highways leading to stations or termini of steam communications have increased in their traffic'.[9] Road carriers such as Pickfords shifted their attention to connecting trips to the railways, rather than taking goods over longer distances. Pickfords already had associations with the Holyhead road: they had set up a branch in Markyate, in Hertfordshire, in the late eighteenth century, and a road there was renamed Pickford Road instead of the arguably more romantic Cheverells Lane.

Generally, the railways had less impact on freight than on passenger journeys. And the mix of means of transport did not just apply to humans – a pedigree cow from Cound near Shrewsbury made its way to London covering three miles on foot, seven by cart, 50 by boat, and 100 miles by railway.[10]

Local carriers, often quite small concerns, could serve a number of purposes: taking people from the village to the local town; collecting goods for the village shop; taking produce to town; and acting as a small and embryonic bus service.[11] The number of commercial road vehicles more than doubled between 1811 and 1851, and then did so again by 1881.[12]

Some types of journey also required road transport. Visitors to Snowdonia could take the train as far as Betws-y-Coed from 1868,

[9] Quoted in Bagwell and Lyth, 2002.
[10] Information at Attingham Park.
[11] Research into travel in Leicestershire, quoted in Barker and Gerhold, 1993.
[12] Quoted in Barker and Gerhold, 1993.

but the line then headed north to Llandudno, so they would have to take the road to see the mountains either east or west. Prominent among those visitors in the mid-nineteenth century were artists, and one of the leaders was David Cox, who was born just off the Holyhead road in Deritend, Birmingham, in 1783. Cox gradually extended his range of work, making annual trips to Betws-y-Coed, staying in the Royal Oak Hotel, from 1844 onwards. He was the leading light in an artists' colony that worked there each summer until 1856. A stretch of wood running alongside the River Llugwy, heading towards Swallow Falls, is known as Artists Wood. Walking through the wood, with the Holyhead road a little way above you to the left, and the river just below sparkling in the sunshine, it's easy to transport yourself into a scene like Cox's *Near Betws y Coed*, for example.

Figure 36 Artists Wood, Betws-y-Coed

Rail travel also had a big impact on the townscapes around the road, as well as on the countryside. In the mid-eighteenth century, according to John Roque's map, Paddington, near to the Roman route out of London, was a little village, with St Mary's church in the middle of the Green. The artist William Hogarth and his beloved, Jane Thornhill, eloped there to get married. More intensive development had been sparked by the building of the Grand Junction Canal, and this was given a further shot in the arm when Paddington station opened in 1838, designed by Isambard Kingdom Brunel. The station is very close to the old Watling Street, and the extra building and activity nearby made the area more cosmopolitan, as it remains. Elsewhere, of course, commerce fell away as a result of the railways, and many coaching inns did not survive, at least as inns – one of the main examples in Shrewsbury, the Talbot, was turned into premises occupied by the police and the Inland Revenue.

One village on the road took a unique approach to developing its identity. Pwllgwyngyll was the medieval name of a village in Anglesey a few miles from the Menai Bridge, which dates back to the Neolithic era. By the nineteenth century, it was known as Llanfair Pwllgwyngyll – meaning 'St Mary's church [in the township named] hollow of the white hazel'. It was a significant point on the Holyhead road, and it has the finest surviving toll house, with the board showing the tolls intact.

In 1860, however, villagers decided to expand the name, with a view to making it the longest name of any railway station in the country, and extended it to Llanfairpwllgwyngyllgogerychwyrndrobwllllantysiliogogogoch – 'St Mary's church in the hollow of the white hazel near to the rapid whirlpool of Llantysilio of the red cave'.

The name is still proudly used on the station platform.

It's not universally understood – when I asked someone in the village emporium about the origin, they didn't know. But maybe it works in attracting tourists: we saw eight coaches parked outside!

Llanfair PG has a further, if less obvious, distinction – in 1915, it became the first place in Britain to have a branch of the Women's Institute.

Figure 37 Station name at Llanfair PG

Figure 38 Bird's Custard factory, Birmingham

The development of the canals had been a vital building block for the Industrial Revolution, and rail transport added to the pace of change. Many businesses chose also to set up on the main roads.

Alfred Bird selected Deritend in Birmingham for his factory making the famous custard powder in the 1840s. The product was very successful, and continued to be made on the site until 1964.

A few miles to the east, in Hay Mills, is the Webster and Horsfall factory, which is still going strong, making steel wire on the Coventry Road. It has a particular significance for me in that my uncle spent his working life there. It has a wider significance in the development of international communications. The Websters had been active in developing different types of steel wire from the early eighteenth century, and their partnership with James Horsfall, an expert in heat treatment, enabled the firm to manufacture a superior product whose uses included the first transatlantic telegraph cable, laid in 1866. A century later, Webster and Horsfall supplied a very specialist suspension cable to support Ireland's only cable car, which connects Dursey Island to the Beara Peninsula in County Cork. It's more than likely that supplies, spares and advisers travelled from Birmingham via Holyhead as part of both these historic projects.[13]

Nearby was another historic manufacturing site, BSA, which stood for Birmingham Small Arms. Founded in 1860, it won a lot of government contracts, and by the late 1860s was reckoned to be the biggest armament company in the world.[14] It supplied Lewis guns in the First World War, and Lee Enfield rifles in the Second. Towards the end of the nineteenth century,

[13] I am grateful to my cousins, John Hudson and Paul Hudson, for help with this section.
[14] www.oldbritishguns.com/birmingham-small-arms.

it also embarked very seriously on a new line: the manufacture of bicycles.

The need for industrial raw materials shaped the landscape along some stretches of the road. The factories and workshops of Birmingham, Coventry and the Black Country depended on coal from North Warwickshire and South Staffordshire. There had for some time been a pit at Brownhills, and others at Cheslyn Hay and Great Wyrley. Between 1850 and 1870, many new pits opened north of Watling Street, mainly due to two enterprising colliers, William Harrison and John Robinson McClean. By the 1870s, more mining companies were starting work near the Cannock area.

We have an eyewitness report of how this part of the road looked at the turn of the nineteenth century. Charles Harper, writing in 1902, describes the area near Cannock as 'a coal-getting neighbourhood, and the crash of waggons, the shrieking of engines, and coal-dust everywhere bedevil the scene'. He liked Brownhills even less, calling it:

> that abomination of desolation […] a wide, dreary stretch of common land, surrounded by the scattered, dirty, and decrepit cottages of a semi-savage population of nail-makers and pitmen, with here and there a school, a woe-begone brick chapel, a tin tabernacle and a plentiful sprinkling of public houses […] as brown, wiry and innutritious as it is possible for grass to be and with an extraordinary wealth of scrap iron, tin clippings, broken glass, and brickbats deposited over every square yard'.[15]

In comments later about Bilston, in the Black Country, Harper makes clear who he holds to blame for this sort of landscape: 'Here,

---

[15] Harper, 1902.

in these barren and absolutely unproductive wastes, the cynical selfishness of the landed class is abundantly evident.'[16]

Raw material extraction was also important in Wales. Between Chirk Bank and Corwen, the road was used to transport coal and limestone, and on Anglesey itself, the coal mines at Malltraeth Marsh received a boost from the easier transport link.[17] But the main mining site was Bethesda, where slate dominates the landscape. At the end of the nineteenth century, the Penrhyn slate quarry near Bethesda was the biggest in the world, employing 3000 men and shaping the town nearby. Even though the mining operation is much smaller, the contrast is stark, driving along the road, between the beauty and open spaces of Snowdonia and the rows of small dark cottages in Bethesda, only five miles further on, built functionally for the slate workers. Looking across the town from the high vantage point of the church, the foothills of Snowdonia rise up from the outskirts, with magnificent peaks in the distance, but the foreground is of slate-grey roofs on slate-grey houses, sometimes of course under a slate-grey sky. Harper again sympathises with the workers:

> the generations of quarrymen who have laboured to enrich Lord Penrhyn and his ancestors are doomed to dwell in a most squalid place, within sight of some of the most beautiful scenery in the world.

Penrhyn remains the biggest slate quarry in Britain, but only about 200 people work there now.

Alongside business people and their staff, the travellers along the Holyhead road included two of the major political

[16] Harper, 1902.
[17] Quartermaine, 2003.

figures of the century. Sir Robert Peel was MP for Tamworth from 1830 to 1850, and made his home at Drayton Manor, near the town. In the 1820s, Peel achieved perhaps his best-known innovation, in introducing the modern police force, whose officers were sometimes nicknamed 'peelers' in tribute. In 1834, he was asked by King William IV to be Prime Minister, and promptly launched the Tamworth Declaration, a manifesto which effectively provided much of the policy thinking behind the Conservative Party. In his second stint as Prime Minister, he abolished the Corn Laws. He continued to live in Tamworth after his political career came to an end, and became president of the Tamworth Farmers Club – the Tamworth breed of pig originated on his estate.

One of Peel's eventual successors as leader of the Conservative Party, Benjamin Disraeli, was MP for Shrewsbury from 1841 to 1847.

Disraeli also visited Castle Bromwich, where I lived as a small child, later on in his career when he was Prime Minister, to see Lady Bradford at Castle Bromwich Hall. As a result, Castle Bromwich was apparently the first Post Office outside London to have a telephone line installed, so that Disraeli could attend to government business. The building served as a post office until 2004 but is now a hairdressing salon.

Travel for pleasure grew in the nineteenth century. George Borrow gives us a picture of travel in Wales in the middle of the century, including from a walk he took from Llangollen to Bangor, while his wife and daughter went by train. After slaking his thirst in the Owen Glendower inn in Corwen, he heads for Cerrig-y-Drudion, and after five miles finds 'a kind of looking place [...] doubtless made by the proprietor of the domain for the use of admirers of scenery [...] for some time [I] enjoyed one of the wildest and most beautiful scenes imaginable.'

Borrow had his own way of introducing himself. When he got to the Lion Inn at Cerrig-y-Drudion, he bowed to 'a stout, comely, elderly lady', and said:

> Madam, as I suppose you are the mistress of this establishment, I beg leave to inform you that I am an Englishman, walking through these regions, in order fully to enjoy their beauties and wonders. I have this day come from Llangollen, and being somewhat hungry and fatigued, hope I can be accommodated here with a dinner and a bed.

Fortified, he walked on through Pentrefoelas to the Vale of Conway, 'to which in the summer time fashionable gentry from all parts of Britain resort for shade and relaxation'. As he headed up to the pass towards Capel Curig, he came upon 'neat dwellings for the accommodation of visitors with cool apartments on the ground floor [...] within them I observed tables, and books, and young men, probably English collegians, seated at study'.

Borrow was in good company in visiting Capel Curig. Queen Victoria stayed there, and the Capel Curig Hotel was renamed the Royal Hotel in about 1870 in her honour. The hotel was rewarded in that her three successors, Edward VII, George V and Edward VIII, all followed her example. It became an outdoor pursuits centre in 1955, but retained a royal link – it's called Plas y Brenin, which means King's Place.

Borrow liked his hotel, which he calls 'a very magnificent edifice', where he 'dined in a grand saloon amidst a great deal of fashionable company'.

We don't know whether Borrow stayed in the Royal Hotel, or perhaps at the nearby Tyn-y-Coed hotel, which makes no secret of its attachment to its coaching past: a full-size replica of a stagecoach, painted bright yellow and blue, stands proudly outside, in full view of the road.

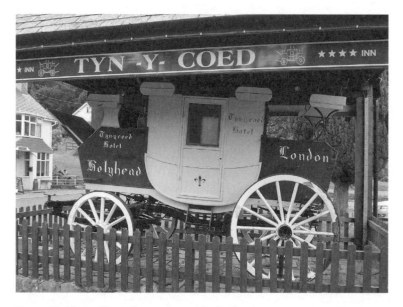

Figure 39 Tyn-y-Coed, the coach outside the hotel

Queen Victoria's long reign coincided with a period when roads were less important in getting people around than before or since. She came to the throne in 1837, just as the railways were being established. For much of the next six decades, rail was the obvious choice for long journeys, and the road suffered. The historian of Roman roads, Thomas Codrington, writing around 1900, reports that 'from the crossroads from Ashby St Leger to Crick, Watling Street is now grassed over for two and a half miles'. Nonetheless, road travel remained important, and towards the end of the century, new options opened up.

In the 1860s, the Coventry Sewing Machine Company became aware of a French invention, a two-wheeled, pedal-powered machine, known as a 'velocipede', and began making a few. As the bicycle developed in factories near the Holyhead road, it became more affordable and popular – half a million were in use by 1890.

More people in Coventry were employed making cycles than in any other industry, with 4,000 workers spread across more than 70 companies, including some who were to become great names in motor manufacture, such as Humber and Triumph.

Bikes enabled many more people to travel independently, at least for short distances. But by the time Queen Victoria died in 1901, an even bigger game changer had arrived.

Chapter 9

The Advent of the Motor Car: From Edwardian Pioneers to 1950s Mass Travel

Richard was less interested in the bank than in the road, the magnificent artery which stretches, almost in a straight line, from the Marble Arch to Chester. Truly the Roman builders of that road had a glorious disregard of everything save direction. Up hill and down dale the mighty Watling Street travels, but it never deviates. After sixty years of disuse, it had resumed its old position as a great highway through the magnificence of England. The cyclist and the motorist had rediscovered it, rejuvenating its venerable inns, raising its venerable dust, and generally giving new vitality to the leviathan after its long sleep.

—*Teresa of Watling Street*, Arnold Bennett, 1904

In 1898, the manager of a company making machines for sheep shearing drove his three-wheeled prototype car from Birmingham to Rhyl and back – a journey of some 250 miles – without a breakdown. His name was Herbert Austin, and the car was named after his company, Wolseley. Austin would have taken in at least part of the Holyhead road. As well as testing out his vehicle – which

was described in *The Engineer* magazine as being like a bath chair[1]
– he was blazing a trail that millions would follow, as car ownership
transformed society, and the road system and landscape with it.

There had been little success in devising new motor-powered
road vehicles in the nineteenth century. One reason was the Red
Flag Act of 1865. This Act has become notorious for requiring a
man with a flag to walk in front of the early motor cars: in fact, it
went back to the days when traction engines were in development,
and the supporters of the railway and horse-power industries were
able to block them.[2]

The motor car proved harder to resist. In the winter of 1885–
86, a German named Karl Benz built a two-seater tricycle powered
by a gas engine, and this is usually seen as the invention of the
motor car as we know it. Within a few months, Daimler and
Maybach had built the first four-wheel petrol engine car, and the
earliest production vehicles followed in 1888.[3] By the end of the
century, there were around 700–800 cars on the roads in Britain.[4]

The Holyhead road played host to much of the early activity,
in the Coventry area. Two entrepreneurs, Frederick Simms and
H J Lawson, bought the UK rights to Daimler's technology, and
found premises in Coventry to build the first production car in the
UK. Other manufacturers followed suit. Many of these moved into
making cars: for example, the Rover name goes back to a 'Rover'
safety bicycle designed by J K Starley in 1885, and Starley's firm
produced Rover motorcycles in 1903 before moving on to cars the
following year.

Some of these early producers became household names,
which were certainly still current when I was growing up in the

[1] www.uniquecarsandparts.com.au.
[2] Davies, 2006.
[3] www.nationalmotormuseum.org.uk/timeline.
[4] Parker, 2013.

1960s. Humber made the transition from bikes to cars, and moved all their production to Coventry by 1908. Hillman made the same move via motorcycles. And Alvis, which made sportier models from the 1920s, actually had their premises on the Holyhead Road itself in Coventry.[5]

Twenty miles further west, Herbert Austin was setting up the Wolseley Motors factory in Birmingham, initially making luxury cars, before setting up his own Austin Motor Company in Longbridge. Other factories sprang up along the road: Joseph Sankey and Sons, which had started up in Bilston, became the largest maker of car wheels in Europe, with a factory near Wellington in Shropshire.[6]

By the start of the Second World War, the traveller along the Holyhead road would have passed plenty of manufacturing plants, many of them linked to motor vehicles. At the London end, Cricklewood – today, mostly a residential and retail area – had a Bentley Motors factory. It was also the site of the Handley Page Aircraft Company, which took advantage of the Cricklewood Aerodrome. Nearby, Cricklewood Studios was the largest in the country at the time. The Triumph Motorcycle factory was at Meriden, until its demise in the late 1980s. Heading into Birmingham, BSA, best known for the (Birmingham) Small Arms that gave it its name, produced large quantities of motorcycles at its Coventry Road factory well into the twentieth century.

This increase in manufacturing was in response to public demand. The sense of excitement at the power of the motor car was perhaps best captured by a rather unlikely driver:

Glorious, stirring sight! [...] The poetry of motion! The *real* way to travel. The *only* way to travel! Here today – in next week

[5] Ibid.
[6] Morrison and Minnis (2012).

tomorrow! Villages skipped, towns and cities jumped – always somebody else's horizon!

So said Mr Toad in *The Wind in the Willows*.[7]

Toad may have got into trouble for stealing a car, but vehicle ownership by legitimate means was rising fast. The number of cars licensed rose from less than 10,000 in 1904, to about 130,000 by the start of the First World War. By the early 1920s, car ownership was heading for 250,000, overtaking the number of motorbikes at about that point, and it continued to rise sharply, to reach nearly 2 million shortly before the start of the Second World War.[8]

One of the reasons for this growth was that prices were falling. A 1904 Rover for two people, made at the New Meteor Works in Coventry, would have cost £120 when new, though that was roughly a year's salary for a teacher. It was advertised, in a way which would not pass muster these days, as 'the most reliable and cheapest car in the world – A LADY CAN DRIVE IT'.

A car costing £500 in 1922 fell to £325 four years later – in today's prices, that's a fall from £24,800 to £17,300.[9] Herbert Austin had a major hand in this: the development of the Austin 7, launched in 1922 for just £165, helped to bring motoring within reach of people who could not previously afford it, in the way that the Ford Model T did in the USA. Nearly 300,000 were produced before production was finally wound up in 1939. Car manufacturers also began to offer financing packages in the 1920s.

For the majority who still couldn't afford a car, bus services grew: London had only twenty buses in 1905, but a thousand three years later. In the Midlands, the Birmingham and Midland Motor Omnibus Company was formed in 1904. As it expanded its services, it headed off a potential conflict with Birmingham

---

[7] Kenneth Grahame's classic work first appeared in 1908.
[8] Dyos and Aldcroft, 1971, Davies, 2006, and Carnevali and Strange, 2014.
[9] Converted using the Bank of England inflation calculator.

Figure 40 My Grandad's Austin 10, pictured in about 1939. The child in front is my mother.

Corporation by striking a deal that Midland Red would operate services from outside Birmingham into the city, and the Corporation run services within, some of them organised by my dad's father, who spent his working life there.[10] So it was that in 1969, to cover the ten miles from home in Castle Bromwich (in Warwickshire) to school in Edgbaston (in Birmingham), I caught a Midland Red bus into town, and a yellow Corporation bus out the other side.

The growth of vehicle ownership and road use had implications for government as well as commercially. With the exception of Parnell and the Holyhead road in the early nineteenth century and maybe the military roads in Scotland, the development of the roads had been a low priority for both central and local government. Measures periodically needed to be taken, to try to speed up progress or to ensure safety, but it was rarely at the centre of public

---

[10] Dyos and Aldcroft, 1971.

concern, and hence of political attention. Indeed, commenting on the establishment of the Central Road Board in 1910, one recent book notes: 'This was an important innovation. Since the departure of the Romans in 410 AD, central government had had no responsibility for the main roads'.[11]

The advent of the motor car changed that. After the First World War, the Ministry of Transport was created, and the road numbering system was introduced. The numbers were allocated clockwise from the London to Edinburgh road, which became the A1. The Holyhead road, in pretty much its present guise, became the A5, in the wedge between the A4 running to Bath and the A6 to Carlisle.

After centuries of ad hoc building and patching, road development took a higher priority. The year 1909 saw the creation of a special Road Fund, financed by duty on vehicles and on petrol. From the early days, however, motorists felt short-changed: by 1920, for example, these taxes brought in £20m, but only some £7m was spent on the roads, and mostly on repairs rather than new construction. As so often happens, the growth in traffic outstripped the development of the roads. In a 'Report on London Traffic' published in 1938, a top Transport official, Sir Charles Bressey, said that there was a bottleneck on average every mile between London and Birmingham.[12] By that time, the Ministry of Transport had finally taken responsibility for trunk roads, in 1936.[13]

The development of the road also brought changes to the surrounding landscape. In some places, bypasses appeared – for example, a three-lane bypass was built around Barnet in 1927.[14] And

[11] Bagwell and Lyth, 2002.

[12] Referred to in Dyos and Aldcroft, 1971. Bressey was Chief Engineer for Roads at the Ministry of Transport, 1921–38, and then President of the Institution of Chartered Surveyors. One of the people who helped with the report was the architect, Sir Edwin Lutyens.

[13] Barker and Savage, 1974.

[14] VCH Middlesex Vol. 5, at www.british-history.ac.uk.

the greater ease of transport, both by road and rail, brought new areas into play for housing. At much the same time as the Barnet bypass, the London County Council built a large new estate of 4000 homes just off the A5 in north-west London, known as the Watling Estate.

The car and the bus made travel more flexible for millions of people, both for work and for leisure. Standing in the centre of Shrewsbury one evening in 1927, the writer and traveller H V Morton observed:

> Every omnibus stage holds a crowd of country people burdened with parcels. The baskets which they brought to market full of cheese or butter or eggs are now full of other things – gramophone records and ribbons, wireless valves, the best Sunday pair of lisle thread stockings, and a new knitted tie for dad! [...] They stand patiently waiting for the homeward charabanc that has done more than anything since the railway train to alter English country life, and has done it more effectually, by bringing the possibility of the town not to some distant station, but right to the end of a country lane.[15]

Morton had mixed feelings about the explosion in travelling. On the plus side:

> The popularity of the cheap motor-car is also greatly responsible for this long-overdue interest in English history, antiquities, and topography. More people than in any previous generation are seeing the real country for the first time.

This had its downsides, however:

> The danger of this, as every lover of England knows, is the vulgarisation of the countryside. I have seen charabanc parties from the large manufacturing towns [...] behaving with a barbaric lack of manners.

[15] Morton, 1927.

But he ended on a positive note:

> Against the vulgarisation of the country, we must place to the
> credit of this new phase in the history of popular travel the fact
> that thousands of intelligent men and women are every year
> discovering the countryside for themselves.

Before the car and the charabanc, the bicycle had begun to open
up more of the countryside to touring, and the car extended that
opportunity – whole families could travel together, and decide for
themselves which routes to explore. This was reflected in facilities
along the way. One of the earliest petrol stations was at Blue Boar
Corner, near Dunchurch. This was named after Blue Boar Lake –
legend has it that a blue boar lived there in Robin Hood's day. The
name migrated later to the motorways: the Blue Boar company
were the first owners of the Watford Gap service station a few
miles away on the M1.

Fuel for the travellers themselves was provided partly by inns,
which developed to meet the emerging demand, and partly by a
new generation of teahouses, which were popular in the 1930s.
In the early part of the century, a move to revive country inns
was led by Earl Grey.[16] He set up a countrywide network of
Public Trust House Companies to refurbish old inns, and the
first, in 1904, was the Waggon and Horses at Ridge Hill on the
Holyhead road between Barnet and St Albans. The inns became
part of the Trusthouse Forte empire, though this particular one was
demolished to make way for the M25.[17]

For overnight stays, a new chain of roadhouses emerged,
called the Knights of the Road, built to a standard design. Again,

---

[16] This was the 4th Earl Grey. The tea is associated with the 2nd Earl Grey.
Sir Edward Grey, Foreign Secretary in the run-up to the First World War, was a
distant relation.
[17] Morriss, 2004.

Coventry was the pioneer, launching the first Knight in 1932, and Hinckley was among the next wave a few months later.[18] This building won praise for its design. At its opening, one of the speakers, Leslie Goodwin, spoke of 'the complete contrast it represented as compared with many of the comfortless old-fashioned early Victorian hotels in which many had previously been accommodated'. He also struck an international comparison:

> As far as building was concerned this country was behind the Spaniard, who was perhaps the most brilliant builder in the world. These houses should do much to improve the architecture of the British house of accommodation.[19]

The Hinckley Knight remains in its original location on Watling Street, now part of the Flaming Grill chain.

Figure 41 Hinckley Knight restaurant

[18] Morrison and Minnis, 2012.
[19] Website: The Buildings of Hinckley, Hinckley.netfirms.com.

Some of the more traditional hotels are still in place as well. I picked up in a secondhand shop a copy of the *Automobile Association Hotel Handbook* 1938–39. This proudly displays the association's telephone number on the front cover – Whitehall 1200, not far from the renowned number for the Metropolitan Police HQ at Scotland Yard, which was Whitehall 1212. Among the recommended hotels are the two where I stayed with my mother when researching this book: the Mytton and Mermaid, at Atcham, near Shrewsbury, would have cost us between 8 and 10 shillings (40–50 pence) each for single rooms, and 5 shillings (25 pence) for dinner; the George in Lichfield charged about the same for dinner, but rooms were a bit cheaper.

As people began to travel more, as well as refreshment they needed maps to guide them. The mapping industry duly grew, and one of the most graphic examples was Pratts High Test Plan of Watling Street, part of a series produced in the 1930s. It's an engaging document, a cross between map and travel guide. The mood is set by cartoons of 'A Roman Triumph on Watling Street', and 'The Canterbury Pilgrims', but the directions and distance information give the traveller what's needed to plan the journey.

The plan shows the whole country, but majors on a corridor either side of Watling Street, all the way from Dover to Holyhead. It takes the traveller out of London along the current A5, but the first place named outside London is Barnet, a dog-leg to the east. It has a few descriptions, including: 'Towcester, The Pomfret Arms [this is a Dickens Inn]', and 'Weedon, Once a Royal retreat'. The colours and diagrams certainly make me feel like getting in the car and starting to explore again.

Weedon Bec has become known for another development of the 1930s. The first demonstration of radar took place a few miles to the south, on 26 February 1935. Radio waves were sent from the

Figure 42 Pratt's High Test Plan of Watling Street

Borough Hill transmitter in Daventry, and Arnold 'Skip' Wilkins and Robert Watson Watt set up equipment in a field just off the A5 towards Litchborough, and were able to detect a bomber plane from RAF Heyford, eight miles away.

The Second World War created a pause in the progress of private motoring. Petrol rationing meant that my grandad's Austin Ten stayed in the garage in Hall Green, Birmingham, throughout the War. My mother nicknamed it Mabel, after a line of Frederick's in *The Pirates of Penzance* – when charged to do something by his young lady, he replies:

Beautiful Mabel – I would if I could, but I am not able.[20]

---

[20] *The Pirates of Penzance* is an operetta by Gilbert and Sullivan (G&S). My parents met through the Birmingham G&S Society, and I'm a fan too.

The War may have put an end to motoring for many, but road links were a factor in some crucial decisions. In late August 1938, a shooting party led by a Captain Ridley made their way from London, presumably travelling along Watling Street for at least part of the way, to a country house in the north of Buckinghamshire. The shooting was a cover story: their real purpose was to see if Bletchley Park would work as a wartime location for intelligence activity. Transport links all round were critical to their decision to place the codebreakers there: close to London via Watling Street and via Bletchley station, and close to Oxford and Cambridge. There was also a Post Office repeater station at Fenny Stratford, which made it easy to lay the dedicated cables needed – the magneto route for more regular communications ran overhead on either side of Watling Street.[21]

The War recast some places along the road for ever. Most notable of these was Coventry. H V Morton described it in 1927 as 'a modern manufacturing city which is spread like thick butter over a slice of medievalism'. He continued:

> It is a lucky city. Fire, which wiped old London from the map,
> has spared to Coventry several of the finest buildings of their
> kind in the world.

Within a few years the luck was to run out: the Nazis destroyed most of the city centre, including the medieval cathedral, and killed over 1200 people.

The job of replacing buildings took priority for resources immediately after the War. But as the reconstruction gathered pace, travel picked up again. One notable journey on the A5, presumably by car, involved Roger Bannister, when he was preparing to run the first sub-four-minute mile in 1954. The spiked shoes he wore for this historic achievement were made in Towcester by George

---

[21] www.bletchleypark.org.uk and personal visit to the site.

Law, who had a house with a shop at 174 Watling Street. The story goes that Law didn't have his own scales, so the shoes were taken repeatedly down the road to the local greengrocers to be weighed as Law tried different ways of making the shoes lighter. He made shoes for many other runners, and added rugby boots to his repertoire later in his career.[22]

With car ownership rising from 2.5 million pre-War to around 4 million by 1955, the road system found itself under ever more pressure. And according to the magazine *Picture Post*, nowhere was the pressure heavier than on the A5 between St Albans and Brownhills.

> This is the most vital trunk road in Britain and the busiest commercial highway in Europe. For heavy traffic leaving London, it is not only the Birmingham Road – it is the Liverpool Road, the Manchester Road, the Glasgow Road. In every day and night, over 10,000 vehicles struggle over its southern hundred miles.[23]

So wrote Trevor Philpott in 1955. But this traffic was not a source of pride. Under the heading 'The Road to Disaster: A Judgment on the A5', he continued:

> every mile is fraught with delay, danger, and death.

In places – he cites Markyate, where the bypass did not arrive until 1955 – the road was no more than 16 feet across, quite possibly narrower than in Roman times. And at its widest, it was a three-lane highway, with all the dangers that brought. What he calls 'the main artery of the nation' was 'a hardening artery, [...] in which the flow of life-blood is slowing day by day'.

[22] Sutherland and Webb, 1995.
[23] Philpott, 1955.

These dangers were borne out by a resident of Fazeley, further north. Maureen Sanderson reminisces that 'in those days you took your life in your hands coming out of Mill Lane – the exit was right outside the butchers shop onto the Watling Street.'[24]

Trevor Philpott was clear on the solution: his last page is headed 'The Motorway we MUST Build'. *Picture Post* was adding its voice to a growing clamour for better high roads. As it turned out, they wouldn't have long to wait.

[24] www.fazeley.info

Chapter 10

The Motorways Change
the Game Again

I sometimes dream, perhaps it is only a dream, that in addition to
railways and tramways, we may see great highways constructed for
rapid motor traffic, and confined to motor traffic.[1]
—Arthur Balfour, 1905

For half a century, it looked as though the future Prime Minister
Arthur Balfour's dream might remain a dream, but by the 1950s
the need became ever stronger, and the building of our motorway
network began. The first stretch to come into use was actually
a short section of what is now the M6 near Preston, opened by
Harold Macmillan in December 1958. But the first full motorway
to open was the M1, starting with a 55-mile section running
parallel to the A5 from Luton to Crick. Nearly 2000 years on from
the building of Watling Street, again the route north-west out of
London was blazing the trail. Construction began on 24 March 1958.

I was just two days old, so by the time I was aware of the routes
we took from home near Birmingham to London – in our case
travelling to seaside holidays in Kent – we were able to use the

[1] Quoted in Morrison and Minnis, 2012.

M1 instead of the A5, though the road to the motorway, via the Stonebridge roundabout, followed the old coaching route.

The motorway was opened in October 1959, to huge excitement – people went on special day trips on London Transport buses. Before long, this initial euphoria turned into more practical consideration of how the new transport links could be exploited.

Better roads facilitated a new type of development along the Holyhead road. New Towns were a feature of post-war planning, and ten had been designated in the 1940s. By the 1960s, a new generation of planners and politicians were devising further developments. The biggest of these by far was on the A5 in Buckinghamshire, around the established town of Bletchley, but taking its name from a small village nearer the centre of the development, Milton Keynes. Nearly 90 miles further up the Holyhead road, the working title for a new town between Shrewsbury and Wolverhampton was Dawley New Town, after one of the bigger settlements. It eventually came into being as Telford.

Milton Keynes was the first place in the UK to be designated a new city, in 1967.[2] The original proposal may have had the unromantic name of 'North Bucks New City' but did not lack in ambition. The New City was conceived not as a satellite or overspill town but as a new city in its own right. Many of the founding fathers are justly celebrated around the city today – Campbell Park, for instance, is named after the first chairman of the Development Corporation. Another of those involved in the early days gained renown for other reasons. The Minister at the time, Richard Crossman, recorded a visit in his diary in March 1966:

> I spent the whole day in Buckinghamshire selling the idea of our New Town to the seven local authorities concerned. Not unnaturally it was a useful piece of electioneering for Bob

[2] Hill, 2005.

Maxwell, the local Member [of Parliament], and I found the atmosphere fairly good.[3]

Bob Maxwell had a shortish political career as Labour MP for Buckingham (1964–70), but became a household name as Robert Maxwell, owner of Mirror Group newspapers, until he was found dead, engulfed by scandal, when he fell overboard from his yacht in 1991.

Telford had a more difficult birth, with a lot of reviews and changes of mind over the area to be included in the New Town and over its governance. The original plan, reflected in the name Dawley New Town, was to focus on an area south of the A5. The concept was to combine provision for overspill housing for Birmingham and Wolverhampton with regeneration of an area blighted by the decline of its mining and ironworking industries. But debate raged about its size and about the relationship to the wider West Midlands.

Crossman had visited this area too, in August 1965, and recorded his thoughts in characteristically trenchant fashion:

> I had to persuade the corporation to accept the idea that the area designated to them was the wrong one and that we should have a completely new New Town area, including Oakengates and Wellington, and probably a new name.

Crossman moved on to another ministerial post the following year, and it was his successor, Anthony Greenwood, who took the final decision to designate the wider area, including Wellington and Oakengates. He also chose the name. He was a student of industrial history, and his two heroes were Brunel and Telford: since Brunel already had a university to his name, and Telford was more closely associated with Shropshire, Greenwood plumped for

[3] Crossman, 1975. Robert Maxwell was Labour MP for Buckingham well before the scandals over his stewardship of the Mirror Group. Richard Crossman's diaries are particularly significant for me, as reading them got me interested in government, where I made my career.

Figure 43 Telford, Statue of Thomas Telford

him. His statue shows him looking benevolently over the town from its rather fine civic centre.

After this inauspicious start, the town grew rapidly in the 1970s, but was then badly affected by the recession of the early 1980s. It was also hampered by inadequate road communications: all the traffic from the M6 to Telford itself, and to Shrewsbury and north Wales beyond, had to go along the single-carriageway A5 from Gailey, past Weston Park, to the growing New Town. Finally, on 25 November 1983, the new Transport Secretary, Nicholas Ridley, cut the tape on the last section of the M54, and the New Town had the fast links it needed. Another stretch of the A5 became a local road – in the words of Telford's historian, Maurice de Soissons:

a blessed calm fell on the A5, once congested and accident-prone.[4]

[4] De Soissons, 1991.

The new road did indeed enable more economic development, and new industry started to come to Telford, including from the Far East. Maxell tapes were among the pioneers, followed by Tatung and Ricoh. Telford Development Corporation had invested in a full office in Tokyo, and this was starting to pay off.

Closer to home, the Inland Revenue chose Telford as the headquarters for another programme long in gestation – the computerisation of Pay As You Earn – and took the rare step of naming a couple of office blocks after civil servants, Matheson House after Steve Matheson, and Boyd House after Jim Boyd. I was working as a junior sprog in the department in the 1980s, and while I didn't really know Jim Boyd, I can testify that Steve Matheson had a huge hand in the key project of computerising PAYE. The two buildings still stand today, though I doubt whether many people remember those they are named after.

Telford is now doing better economically, with unemployment currently below the national average, though the satellite towns such as Wellington are not doing so well. The town centre has established itself as the prime shopping location for east Shropshire, and the road network, with plenty of dual carriageways, does the job of getting people around, both in and out of the town, and from one side to another. Thomas Telford is commemorated also at one of the roundabouts, by a sculpture of his maker's mark as an engineer.

The two New Towns are a particular example of how roads both shape an area and are shaped by an area. Existing good communications are part of deciding where to locate a New Town. As they develop, they need ever better roads. The old road through Milton Keynes is still named Watling Street, though it has a number on the city's grid system, too – V4 (V stands for Vertical). It is busy at peak times, taking local traffic to factories and retail parks. The modern A5 is a major dual carriageway, carrying through traffic that doesn't use the motorways to and from the Midlands.

Figure 44 Telford, Telford's 'maker's mark'

One of the most celebrated factories in Milton Keynes has an A5 story all of its own. Marshall Amps has been established in the Bletchley area for nearly half a century now. Its location is the result of a journey in the early 1960s. Jim Marshall founded the company in his garage in west London. As he expanded, he began looking for bigger premises, and his property advisers took him to a site in Birmingham. This didn't quite work for Jim – too far from London, or whatever – so the party travelled back along the A5. Apparently on a whim, Jim stopped the car in the Bletchley area: this felt more like it. He found premises which suited him, and they formed the basis for a very successful enterprise. The firm is now in its third building in the area, and its products have been used by The Who, Led Zeppelin and Deep Purple, among others, some of whom have travelled up this stretch of Watling Street to try out the equipment prior to going live in the big concert venues of the land. Jimi Hendrix visited the previous shop in west London.[5]

Some people like to poke fun or criticism at the New Towns but both Telford and Milton Keynes have plenty of green space, good communications, and history. There are a lot of myths around – for example, so far from being a made-up name, Milton Keynes village is actually mentioned in the Domesday Book under the name 'Middeltone'. As far as the roads are concerned, the grid system is efficient, and behind the dual carriageways, the individual parts of town retain their own character. Rather than lacking green space, all are linked by the 'red routes' for cyclists, walkers and runners, so that you can get from Linford Wood in the north to the large open space of Campbell Park or the National Bowl towards the south without having to cross a major road.

Of course it takes time for any New Town to forge its identity, but Milton Keynes has taken advantage of its location, on both the motorway and the A5 and on the mainline from Euston, to become a regional centre for business, shopping and entertainment. It remains an ambitious and forward-looking city, and the evidence is that businesses and individuals like it there.

More generally, as some writers have observed, is Milton Keynes so very different from many places, and indeed what most people want from their town or city? It offers good transport links, modern houses, mostly with parking, modern facilities in the centre, bigger retail outlets on the outskirts. You can see why the writer Blake Morrison commented, 'This is where most of us live now, in a place vaguely resembling Milton Keynes.'[6]

The stretch of the road between Milton Keynes and Telford reflects the old and the new in the economy and society in different

---

[5] Information from a visit to Marshall Amps, February 2014, and Marshall Amps website.

[6] Newspaper article, quoted in Clapson, 2004.

Figure 45 Brownhills: Statue of a miner

ways. On the outskirts of the town of Brownhills, in Staffordshire, is a 46-feet high statue of a coal miner, made from stainless steel by John McKenna, which was put up in 2006.

The area may not have been as well known for its mines as Yorkshire or Nottinghamshire, but south Staffordshire and north Warwickshire both employed tens of thousands of men in the industry for a century or so. The statue is marking activity that is well in the past: the final mine in Brownhills closed in the 1950s.

Brownhills as a town still has its challenges. Nearby Cannock is doing better, not least with one of the rare manufacturing-related sites on the road: the headquarters of Finning UK, one of the world's largest distributors of Caterpillar products for the construction industry and of power systems, stretches for well over a quarter of a mile along Watling Street in Cannock.

If the Brownhills miner represents the old, the new starts twenty miles or so further east along the road, with the logistics industry. The area around the junction between the M1 and M6 at Catthorpe has turned into a hub for both road and rail movements across the country, and many of the facilities front onto the A5. Magna Park near Lutterworth is one of the biggest distribution centres in Europe – Asda and Argos are among the big firms based there.

One interesting example is the Eddie Stobart soft drinks distribution facility just south of Rugby, which is right on the A5 and has the postal address of Watling Street. It is located so that lorries can easily head a few miles south to the M1 at junction 18, or a few miles north to the M6 at junction 1. It's busy and getting busier – the firm moved a mile or two up Watling Street in search of more space, and continues to grow. The A5 does its job well, they assured me on my visit: not many hold-ups, and an efficient road, though drivers have to be careful as they emerge from the facility onto the main road, especially staff in cars rather than people in big lorries.

There's a bustle about the whole operation. Hundreds of lorries come and go every day, seven days a week, on their way to and from delivering drinks such as Coca-Cola or Britvic fruit juices to the major supermarkets. Some of the drivers stop only for a few minutes, to refuel, or hand in their documents at the end of a shift. Others stay long enough to enjoy a bacon sandwich in the truck stop. A link between Stobarts and a Spanish logistics operation means there are more drivers from abroad up and down the road.

Watching the iconic green lorries come in and out, you get a sense of the nation's economy running. The watching process has also become an end in itself for some. Each Stobart lorry has a

Figure 46 An Eddie Stobart lorry

name on its cab – usually two girls' names together, such as Clare Geraldine, which I saw on its way out. 'There are the spotters,' said one of my hosts, pointing to a couple of guys hanging around the depot with cameras and rucksacks looking for the names on the trucks. Apparently it's a well-established pastime.

In between Brownhills and Daventry is another success story that has adapted to take advantage of changing circumstances. MIRA (now HORIBA MIRA) – which started life as the Motor Industry Research Association – is a large and thriving industrial site, built alongside the A5 near Nuneaton – its postal address is simply Watling Street (Nuneaton). Its origins date back to 1945, and it moved to its present site in 1948, occupying a wartime airfield no longer needed by the military. The location on the A5 was particularly advantageous for the emerging (or re-emerging) motor industry: a Midlands site could service Ford in Liverpool and in Dagenham, and the many Midlands factories in between. MIRA provided facilities for testing roadworthiness, particularly under extreme conditions, and its offering expanded along with the industry itself: the first purpose-built track opened in 1954, followed in 1960 by the world's first purpose-built wind tunnel for the automotive industry. In 1968, a new crash laboratory was opened by the then Minister of Technology, Tony Benn.

Reflecting the fortunes of the car industry, less business came from Birmingham, and more from the likes of Nissan in the North-East, and an increasingly global customer base. MIRA diversified in other ways, working on military vehicles and carrying out a rail crash test. The facilities also played a key part in Britain's sporting life. As well as testing rally cars and vehicles bound for the Le Mans 24-hour race, the cyclist Chris Boardman prepared for his triumph in the 1992 Olympics in the wind tunnel, and more recently Prince Harry and the UK team from Walking With The Wounded prepared for their South Pole Allied Challenge with a 24-hour exercise there, involving snow blizzards, temperatures of -35 degrees centigrade, and winds of up to 200 km/hour.

MIRA continues to develop and grow, capitalising on its central location. GKN, Continental and Goodyear are setting up in the new Technology Centre, and the iconic Aston Martin company of James Bond fame has established a prototype build and testing centre elsewhere on the site.

This expansion has been helped by improvements to the A5 itself, parts of which will be turned into a dual carriageway with improved junctions. In line with today's priorities, there will be better cycle routes too. As so often, developments in the road itself both reflect changes in the economy and also enable further progress. And as often happens, local reactions are mixed. *The Hinckley Times* ran an article in August 2014 headed 'A5 works will mean traffic hell until 2015', but included a comment from Councillor David Bill:

> The resilience of the local economy has been helped by the development of the motorway network, enticing people who want to live here and encouraging new businesses.
> However, one of the major problems has been the inadequacy of the A5 and A47 to cope with all the extra traffic. I have campaigned for years for improvements to keep traffic flowing and now they are coming.[7]

Governments continue to review the strategic road network elsewhere. In north Wales, much of the road development went into the A55 along the coast and the A5 changed little outside the towns. In July 1998, the Welsh Office produced a document saying that the A5 across the mainland would neither be developed as a strategic route nor be part of the core network.[8] As ever, this is good news for some and not for others. Residents of towns along the A5 may be pleased that they have fewer lorries to contend with. On the other hand, the A5 enables thousands of walkers and climbers from the Midlands and beyond to get to Snowdonia for the weekend, and their journeys can be slower and more congested.

A different approach to relieving congestion on the A5, among other roads, was adopted in England in the early 1990s, with the decision to build the M6 relief road through the Midlands as a privately funded venture. Midland Expressway won the concession to run the toll road until 2054, and the road opened in December 2003. In a reminder of the long and rich history of the A5, many Roman artefacts came to light in the course of its construction.

---

[7] www.hinckleytimes.net, 22 August 2014.
[8] Referred to in Quartermaine, 2003.

Driving on the toll road is certainly a different matter from the stop–start frustration that the M6 itself can bring. The M6 Toll website talks about 'stress-free motoring' helped by the chance to stop at 'probably the most pleasurable motorway service station in the country at Norton Canes'. The trouble is that the road is stress-free because not many people use it. If the intention was to entice motorists off the busy M6, it hasn't obviously succeeded, and no further toll motorways have yet been built. But three centuries ago, there was a gap of about fifty years between the first turnpike trust and the second, so things may yet change.

One of the recurring themes of this book is that over time, the road system will adapt with both changes in wider society and changes in technology. It's fair to say that the system hasn't yet adapted as much as other sectors in response to the development of information technology and microelectronics, but there are signs of change – rather than stopping at the toll booth, for example, you can put a tag in your windscreen which enables you to drive straight through, and this has obvious potential for different approaches to charging. Driverless cars are now well into the testing phase. Sections of the M1 and M6 motorways which parallel the Holyhead road are now 'smart motorways', using new technology to vary speed limits in response to driving conditions.

When you look at old photos from the post-War era, the towns look very different but the open road can look much the same. That may not be true over the next half-century.

Chapter 11

The Road Today

Roads go on
While we forget, and are
Forgotten like a star
That shoots and is gone
On this earth 'tis sure
We men have not made
Anything that doth fade
So soon, so long endure.

— 'Roads', Edward Thomas, 1917

The Holyhead road has waxed and waned in importance over the centuries, indeed millennia, of its existence. It continues to change: as I write, the Highways Agency are working on a £160m project to build a new link between the A5 near Dunstable and the M1, designed to reduce congestion and improve safety on the A5, and reduce pressure on the road as it goes through Dunstable town centre. The number of journeys being made had increased, and once the new road is complete, no doubt still more journeys will take place, as tradesmen, parents or shoppers decide that a town is within reach after all.

I said at the start of this book that roads connect and divide, enable journeys and reflect change. The Holyhead road continues to do all four, as it approaches its 2,000th birthday.

Different types of connections are being made, as our reasons for travel evolve. Thankfully, conquest and war are long in the past, with parades on Remembrance Sunday the only time when people in uniform are regularly seen on the road. Long may it stay that way. Journeys linked to faith are still important, but the often long expeditions of Christian pilgrimage have been replaced by shorter journeys to the local place of worship. Both buildings and reasons for travel reflect the local society: in some areas of Birmingham and London, for instance, journeys to Friday prayers will far outnumber those to Holy Communion on a Sunday. Along the stretch of the A5 named the Holyhead Road in Birmingham, Baptists and Wesleyans worship near a Hindu Temple and a Sikh Temple.

Journeys for trade and business continue to be important, of course, but their nature reflects changes in society, too. Alongside the myriad local journeys made, the Midlands section of the A5 reverberates to the sound of huge lorries moving in and out of the many distribution centres, heading for the motorways. But some older practices return in a new guise. Some of the staff at Jack's Hill truckstop on the A5 in Towcester can remember flour from a local mill being delivered direct to customers by horse and cart, and in my grandparents' day, it was common for the grocer to deliver to your home. Those journeys are now mirrored by deliveries from online supermarkets and parcels from Amazon.

Meanwhile, we are travelling more for pleasure. Nationwide, leisure was the most popular reason for car travel in a 2008 survey: 186 trips per person per year, which was double the number of journeys for commuting, and over four times the number of journeys made for shopping.[1]

---

[1] Office for National Statistics, 2010 and 2011.

So new connections are being made, for reasons that are changing. Does the road still divide communities? It is still the administrative boundary between Warwickshire and Leicestershire for twenty miles or so, and between boroughs in London. There are also cultural divides. Local people report a cultural divide between Hinckley, which made hosiery, and Nuneaton, which was a mining area. Some women crossed from south to north to work on the stockings, but not many people went the other way to work in the mining industry.

In Milton Keynes, locals say that visitors, at least, see the big dual carriageways through the city as an obstacle to getting to know the place as a whole, and to linking up the different areas, though in fact doing so is easier than it looks. And it's hard to believe that the building of a major dual carriageway for the A5 east of Shrewsbury in the 1990s, connecting the county town with the M54, had no impact on communications between the communities which found themselves on either side of it, even with bridges over the main road. This hasn't deterred communities the other side of the town from pressing for the section north of Shrewsbury to be made into a dual carriageway, because of the volume of traffic heading for Ireland and north Wales. It is the last remaining stretch of a long-distance route from Felixstowe to Holyhead, designated as a Trans-European Network, which is still single carriageway. A dual carriageway would strengthen connections, and make the main road safer, but it would also divide north Shropshire in new ways.

What is clearer is that road-building or improvement continues to enable change. More roundabouts and dual carriageway in Warwickshire have enabled MIRA to expand efficiently. In Wales, the decision to see the A55 as the trunk road has not done any favours to some businesses on the A5, which is no doubt partly why neighbours in Wales are supportive of the campaign to upgrade the road through Shropshire.

Specific decisions on dualling or bypasses or individual buildings can depend on a number of factors – local politics, the personal preferences of the decision-maker, and so on. But over the medium term, as throughout its history, the road reflects the habits and wishes of the people it serves. So what is the Holyhead road today telling us about this slice of Britain?

I am repeatedly struck by the number of retail outlets and retail parks. Napoleon may have described us as a 'nation of shopkeepers'; today, it can feel more like we are a nation of shoppers. From Cricklewood, five miles from Marble Arch, to the centre of Holyhead, the road is frequently lined by retail parks. Maybe the tide is starting to turn with the advent of internet shopping, though the implications are not positive for all. Tesco had acquired the Royal Hospital site in Wolverhampton, one block south of the Holyhead road, to turn it into a superstore, promising shops, a restaurant and cafe, office and community spaces. But in the face of poor trading results, they dropped the plan in January 2015, as part of a wider retrenchment, to great local anger. It's now set to become housing.

The growth of services is of course a national trend, as is the reduction in manufacturing, sometimes with a direct switch. The former Sankey factory in Bilston, which produced a wide range of metal products from kitchenware to jet engine parts, is now a Morrisons superstore.[2] The BSA factory, with its rich history, is now an Asda.[3] In Coventry, of the large number of factories which flourished for decades in the middle of the twentieth century, only the London Taxi Co survives, now owned by Geely, the Chinese giant which also owns Volvo in Sweden. Jaguar has a small prototype-build and wood veneer facility at their old Browns Lane

[2] http://www.historywebsite.co.uk/Museum/metalware/sankeys/sankey01.htm.
[3] See Chapters 8 and 9.

factory, but the rest have gone, to be replaced by retail parks and distribution warehousing.

Near Holyhead, Anglesey Aluminium Metal Ltd opened in 1971 and was one of the biggest employers in north Wales, but closed in 2009. The Mona industrial park carries on, as a location for smaller firms, and the Alpoco company takes used aluminium products and turns them into powder for the cosmetics industry. The Horizon company are planning a successor to the Wylfa nuclear power station on Anglesey, which could generate significant employment.

There are some exceptions to this picture of ever-reducing manufacturing. Cannock is the headquarters of Finning (UK) Ltd, one of the world's largest distributors of Caterpillar plant and equipment. Between Brownhills and Cannock, Watling Street gives its name to the St Modwen Watling Street Business Park, which was established in around 2000, with tenants ranging from a computer recycling and disposal company to a supplier of antique and reproduction furniture. And I'm delighted to say that Webster & Horsfall, where my uncle worked, is still going strong on the Coventry Road in Birmingham!

Even in our supposedly congested island, there is still plenty of open countryside. The first ten miles or so out of London is all built up, and the old road through the West Midlands conurbation stretches for over twenty miles from Birmingham Airport to Tettenhall. Milton Keynes and Telford are now sizeable places. But apart from these, the 250 miles of road proceed largely through agricultural land in England, and pasture in Wales. Apart from Snowdonia itself, the landscapes are not spectacular in their beauty, but convey a sense of what people think of as England and Wales: a 'green and pleasant land' for England, with undulating countryside, mostly arable, where people live in small towns and villages; in Wales, even greener, with more sheep, more contours, and more stone cottages isolated from smaller settlements.

At the London end, the townscape is completely cosmopolitan. The southernmost stretch near Marble Arch actually has a preponderance of Lebanese stores and cafes, many with Arabic writing above the door rather than traditional British ones. If the Roman soldiers who built the road were to return, they might recognise the Mediterranean fare on offer. The Kilburn High Road includes Irish, Caribbean, African, Middle Eastern and Polish outlets within half a mile. And across the North Circular, where the landscape used to be more traditionally suburban, West Hendon is now changing from having a high Indian population to a greater proportion of Eastern Europeans, with Romanian and Polish shops in Edgware.

This international flavour stops abruptly at the edge of London, to be picked up again in Birmingham, above all as you head through Soho, a few miles north-west of the city centre. Even in a multi-ethnic city, this stretch of road is especially cosmopolitan. Alongside the Pakistani grocers are Kurdish food stores, Turkish restaurants, Polish suppliers, a Romanian mini-market, and a range of fashion emporiums, with Greggs and Iceland representing more traditional British firms. A banner advertising Asian weddings faces an Asian Funeral Director. Some businesses cross cultures: the Chip 'n' Whale shop sells naan bread and curries. Holyhead School has over three-quarters of its students speaking English as an additional language, but that hasn't stopped it being awarded an Outstanding rating from Ofsted, and proudly displaying that on a banner outside.[4]

This is a mile-long street of small shops and small businesses: it's colourful and it's vibrant. Quite abruptly it comes to an end, and more familiar outlets pop up – Halfords and a Drive-thru McDonald's stand more or less opposite the only league football

---

[4] Ofsted website.

ground directly on the route, The Hawthorns, home to West Bromwich Albion.[5]

Even if the physical landscape is only cosmopolitan in a few urban areas, the catering along the road reflects our changing tastes, and our ability as a nation to adapt. Many old-fashioned pubs have simply gone out of business – they stand there as boarded-up corner properties, sometimes with a rotting sign still hanging on, monuments to a way of life which has basically died out. Many others, however, have reinvented themselves. Some are Chinese or Indian restaurants. In London, an old pub is now a restaurant offering Moroccan cuisine and a shisha garden. The Old Crown pub in Digbeth (founded in 1468) has gone in a healthier direction, and has a coffee shop, to appeal to local students.

Other historic buildings have branched out in different ways. The Cock Inn in Kilburn (founded in 1486), once had the Cock Tavern Theatre upstairs, which won awards for fringe-theatre productions. The Bird's custard factory closed in 1964 and became derelict, but has now been reborn as the heart of a creative hub, home to more than 400 businesses with names like Fragile Design and the Apple Pie House. It's also a venue for stag or hen parties. The ensemble is known, simply enough, as The Custard Factory.

Fewer people may go to church, but religious buildings continue to loom large along the road. The medieval parish churches still dominate their villages, thank goodness, while some secular buildings in urban areas are bucking the trend and reflect new styles of worship. In Kilburn, at the bottom of the road where I used to live, the 'National' building, once the largest cinema in Europe, has become a 'HelpCentre' for a Christian organisation, and on the

---

[5] The Hawthorns is the highest stadium above sea level in the football league, so the road at this point is on relatively high ground, about 170m up. The Birmingham City ground is not far off the Coventry road, near the centre of Birmingham.

other side of the road, the old State cinema is now Ruach Ministries. The Islamic Centre of England is half a mile further down the road. In Digbeth, an office block is being used for the Potters House Christian Fellowship Church, and welcomes potential worshippers in Polish and French as well as English.

Sometimes, however, ironic shifts occur in the opposite direction: in the centre of Atherstone, the old Temperance Chapel was for a while a nightclub called Barbarella's. The town of Bethesda was named after the Bethesda chapel. It's a fine building in its way, neo-classical in style, befitting its foundation in 1820: symmetrical either side of a portico with two columns and a pediment above. It must have been an impressive ornament to the growing town in the peak days of slate mining. There is an old sign in Welsh still on display, advertising (I think!) preaching at 10 o'clock and 6 o'clock, with school in between times. But another board announces that in July 1998, it was re-opened by Councillor Ieuan Llewelyn Jones, for North Wales Housing Association Ltd.

Holyhead itself continues to be very busy, with people travelling for all sorts of reasons. Freight traffic is still important, driven by men, and occasionally women, from an ever wider range of countries. Reflecting the trend for some people to work further away from home, employees who live in Wales but work in Ireland take advantage of the Club Class facilities on the 9 o'clock ferry on a Monday morning, to get started on the week's work on the laptop. Cruise ships arrive in increasing numbers, decanting their passengers for trips to local attractions.

Some of the passengers arriving on coach trips beetle off down the road at high speed. When we were in Llangollen, the Hand Hotel was hosting a group of young American visitors. They had breakfast at 7 a.m. (having asked for an even earlier start), on their way to Oxford and then to spend the night in London. Pennant and Borrow might not have approved, but Defoe might have welcomed the speed for some of his journeys.

Figure 47 Holyhead: Welcome to the port

For those wanting to stick to the water, Holyhead has ambitions to build a new marina – there are already a lot of pleasure craft. The sea conditions are favourable, so Holyhead could become one of the prime locations for sailing on the western coast of the UK, bringing more visitors along the road for leisure reasons.

Back on dry land, we were in Stony Stratford, looking for a coffee, and saw a place which appeared to be both a cycle shop and a cafe. Sure enough, the owner explained that cyclists on long bike rides were looking for somewhere they could stop, park their bikes safely, fix any minor mechanical problems, and have a coffee and a cake and put the world to rights – as their forerunners would have done over a beer. Refreshed, they would then undertake the second half of the ride. Straightforward cafes or bike shops didn't quite meet the need, so these new combined premises have emerged. There is one in Redbourn too, called the Hub Coffee Bar and Cyclists Refuge. We can't chalk this up as an example of British ingenuity, as it's apparently copied from the Continent, but it is evidence of continuing adaptability.

So this is the picture the Holyhead road paints of Britain today: a land of variety, cosmopolitan in places, traditional in others; a land of urban congestion and of wide open countryside; where old buildings sit reasonably happily alongside new ones; where ugliness neighbours outstanding beauty; where we buy more than we make. A place that's adaptable.

What will the traveller find in thirty years' time, as the road nears its third millennium? We can be fairly confident of driverless cars, for example, and that the traffic-management technology being rolled out gradually on the motorways will have become more widespread. But what about potential game changers? When Telford persuaded Parliament to invest huge sums in upgrading the road in 1815, neither he nor they could have guessed that thirty years from then, traffic would be migrating rapidly on to the railways, leaving the roads much quieter. Maybe video technology will mean that we don't need to leave our homes much, but can work together in virtual offices, and learn in virtual classrooms, while our goods are delivered by drone rather than by van? But more radically, might we each be able to strap on a personal transportation device and be delivered by air to visit our relations in Birmingham, or to go walking in Snowdonia?

Whatever the outcome, I am confident of two things.

First, the road will continue to adapt, both shaping the world around it and reflecting that world. Almost all journeys will continue to start and finish by road, and the carriageway and the roadscape will evolve accordingly.

Second, there will remain the joy of a journey. There will always be as many reasons for travel as there are travellers. The Holyhead road has seen journeys for conquest, for pilgrimage, for trade, for a new life, as well as to deliver goods, buy them, and take the kids to school. But there will always be those of us who enjoy the journey for its own sake, to experience and understand the country in which we live. In the words of Mr Toad:

> There's real life for you [...] The open road, the dusty highway, the heath, the common, the hedgerows, the rolling downs! Camps, villages, towns, cities! Here today, up and off to somewhere else tomorrow! Travel, change, interest, excitement! The whole world before you, and a horizon that's always changing![6]

[6] Kenneth Grahame, 1908.

Acknowledgements

I'd like to thank the staff at the British Library for the efficient service they provide. I also had interesting conversations with staff in the museums in Towcester, Shrewsbury and Oswestry.

Clare Christian and her team at RedDoor have provided support to a first-time author that has been expert and professional, and also friendly and understanding. Huge thanks to them all. I'm also very grateful to Jo de Vries and Emma Parkin of Conker House Publishing for their advice and help at an earlier stage.

A number of people kindly spent time with me, showing me round their part of the world: my friend David Hill, then chief executive of Milton Keynes Council; Richard Bifield, chairman of the Friends of the Ironbridge Gorge Museum, and an expert on Telford; and in Holyhead, Alan Williams from Stena Port, and John Cave. George Gillespie, chief executive, enabled me to visit MIRA, and Jake Stevenson, general manager, allowed me to go to the Eddie Stobart depot near Rugby. Thanks to them all.

I'm very grateful to a number of friends who have read sections of the book, and given me advice and encouragement. In particular, I'd like to thank a schoolfriend, Stephen Cooper, for invaluable help, general and specific – his *The Final Whistle: The Great War in Fifteen Players* is a great read, as is the follow-up.

My greatest debt is to my wife, Judith. She has come on many of the journeys, added her expertise, critiqued the ideas, and generally lived with the book for a long time.

The book is dedicated to my parents. Sadly, my dad died many years ago: the book would have benefited immensely from his deep knowledge of Birmingham and the West Midlands. Thankfully, my mother is very much alive: the book has benefited immensely from her accompanying me on some of the trips, reading the text, and contributing her deep knowledge of stately homes and gardens, and the people who lived in them. Far more important, they gave me – and still give me – love and support in everything I have done in life.

References

Bagwell, Philip, and Lyth, Peter, *Transport in Britain: From Canal Lock to Gridlock* (London, Bloomsbury, 2002)

Barker, T C and Savage, C I, *An Economic History of Transport in Britain* (London, Hutchinson University Library, 1974)

Barker, T C (ed.), *The Economic and Social Effects of the Spread of Motor Vehicles* (London, Macmillan, 1987)

Barker T C and Gerhold D, *The Rise and Rise of Road Transport* (Cambridge, Cambridge University Press, 1993)

Bede (trans. Sherley-Price), *A History of the English Church and People* (London, 1968)

Beier, A L, *Masterless Men: The Vagrancy Problem in England, 1560–1640* (London, Methuen, 1985)

Beresford, M W and Finberg, H P R, *English Medieval Boroughs: A Hand List* (Newton Abbot, David & Charles, 1973)

Bogart, Dan, 'Did Turnpike Trusts increase transportation investment in 18th-century England?' *Journal of Economic History, Vol. 65, No. 2, , pp. 439–468* (June 2005)

Borrow, George, *Wild Wales: Its People, Language and Scenery* (1854) (online edition: Oxford, MS: 1996)

Britnell, Richard H, *The Commercialisation of English Society, 1000–1500* (Manchester, Manchester University Press, 1996)

Brown, Peter, *Chaucer at Work: The Making of the Canterbury Tales* (Routledge, 1994)

Cameron, K, *English Place Names* (London, Batsford, 1996)

Carnevali, F and Strange, J M (eds.), *20th Century Britain: Economic, Cultural and Social Change* (Routledge, 2014)

Cary, John, *Cary's New Itinerary: or an Accurate Delineation of the Great Roads Both Direct and Cross Throughout England and Wales* (London, 1802)

Champion, W A, 'Topography, 1540–1640' (website: Discovering Shropshire's History, 2006)

Chaucer, Geoffrey, *The Canterbury Tales* (ed Nevill Coghill, London, Penguin Classics, revised edition 1977)

Clapson, Mark, *A Social History of Milton Keynes* (London, Frank Cass, 2004)

Cooper, A, *Bridges, Law and Power in Medieval England 700–1400* (Boydell Press, 2006)

Crossman, R H S, *The Diaries of a Cabinet Minister,* Volume 1 (London, Hamish Hamilton and Jonathan Cape, 1975)

Darby, H C, *Domesday England* (Cambridge, Cambridge University Press, 1977)

Davies, Hugh, *From Trackways to Motorways* (Stroud, Tempus, 2006)

Defoe, Daniel (ed. Pat Rogers), *A Tour Through the Whole Island of Great Britain* (London, Penguin Books, 1971)

Department for Transport, *National Travel Survey* (2015)

De Quincey, Thomas (ed. Barry Milligan), *The English Mail Coach* (pub. 1849) (2003)

De Soissons, Maurice (1991), *Telford: The Making of Shropshire's New Town* (Shewsbury, Swan Hill Press, 1991)

Dickens, Charles, *The Uncommercial Traveller* (1863)

Domesday Book (ed. Morris, John), (Chichester, Phillimore, 1975)

Drayton, Michael, *Poly-Olbion* (London 1613)

Dyos, H J and Aldcroft, D H, *British Transport: An Economic Survey from the Seventeenth Century to the Twentieth* (Leicester University Press, 1971)

Evans, G R, *John Wyclif* (IVP Academic, 2005)

Fiennes, C, *Through England on a Side Saddle in the Time of William and Mary* (London, Field & Tuer, The Leadenhall Press, 1888)

Fiennes, Celia (ed. Christopher Morris), *The Illustrated Journeys of Celia Fiennes 1685–c.1712* (Stroud, Sutton Publishing Ltd, 1995)

Garmonsway, G N (Ed.), *Anglo-Saxon Chronicle* (Dent Dutton, new edition 1972)

Gash N, *Peel* (single-volume edition, London, Longman, 1976)

Gould, Jim, *Letocetum: The Rise and Decline of a Roman Posting Station* (J Gould, 1998).

Grahame, Kenneth, *The Wind in the Willows* (London, Methuen, 1908)

Guldi, Jo, *Roads to Power: Britain Invents the Infrastructure State* (Cambridge Mass. and London Harvard University Press, 2012)

Hadfield, Charles, *Thomas Telford's Temptation: Telford and William Jessop's Reputation* (Baldwin, Cleobury Mortimer, 1993)

Harper, Charles, *The Holyhead Road: The Mail-Coach Road to Dublin* (two volumes, London, 1902)

Harrison, David: *The Bridges of Medieval England: Transport and Society 400–1800* (Oxford, Clarendon Press, 2004)

Harvey, Sally, *Domesday: Book of Judgement* (Oxford, Oxford University Press, 2014)

Higgins, Charlotte, *Under Another Sky: Journeys in Roman Britain* (London, Jonathan Cape, 2013)

Hill, Marion, *Milton Keynes: A History & Celebration* (Salisbury, The Francis Frith Collection, 2005)

Hindle, B P, *Roads, Tracks, and their Interpretation* (London, Batsford, 1973)

Holmes, George, *The Later Middle Ages* (Edinburgh, Thomas Nelson, 1962)

Hooke, Della, *Anglo-Saxon Landscapes of the West Midlands: The Charter Evidence* (British Archaeological Reports, 1981)

Hooke, Della, *England's Landscape: The West Midlands* (English Heritage/Collins, 2006)

House of Commons, Select Committee on the Road from London to Holyhead, various reports (2nd and 3rd reports, 1819)

Hughes, Mervyn, 'Telford, Parnell, and the Great Irish Road', *Journal of Transport History*, Vol. VI, No. 4 (November 1964)

Hughes, Thomas, *Tom Brown's Schoolboys*, 1857 (Project Gutenberg edition)

Hutton, William, *An History of Birmingham*, 1783 (Project Gutenberg edition)

Kind, Alan, 'Inclosure Awards: An Introduction', paper for the National Federation of Bridleway Associations (1999)

Leges, O'Brien, Bruce (Ed.), *Leges Edwardi Confessoris* (12th century), (website: Earlyenglishlaws.ac.uk)

Leland, John (ed. Chandler, John), *Itinerary: Travels in Tudor England* (Stroud, 1993)

Livingston, Helen, *In the Footsteps of Caesar: Walking Roman Roads in Britain* (Dial House, 1995)

Lorenz, Andrew, *GKN: The Making of a Business, 1759–2009* (Wiley, 2012)

Margary, Ivan D, *Roman Roads in Britain* (Third edition, London, John Baker, 1973)

Maitland, F W, *Domesday Book and Beyond* (Cambridge University Press, 1897)

Millea, Nick, *The Gough Map: The Earliest Road Map of Great Britain* (Oxford, The Bodleian Library, 2007)

Miller, Norma, *Tacitus, Annals 14: A Companion to the Penguin Translation* (Bristol, Bristol Classical Press,1987)

Morrison, K A and Minnis, J, *Carscapes* (Yale University Press, 2012)

Morriss, Richard K, *Roads: Archaeology and Architecture* (The History Press, 2004)

Morton, H V, *In Search of England* (London, Methuen, 1927)

Ogilby, John (ed. J B Harley), *Britannia* (Amsterdam, Theatrum Orbis Terrarum Ltd, 1970)

Ogilby, John (ed. Helen Wallis), *Britannia: A Survey of the Roads of England and Wales in 1675* (Leeds, Old Hall Press, 1989)

Ogilby, John, *Itinerarium Angliae: or a book of roads wherein are contained the principal road-ways of His Majesty's Kingdom of England and Dominion of Wales* (London 1675)

Overton, Mark, 'Agricultural Revolution?: England 1540–1850' in *Recent Findings of Research in Economic & Social History* (Economic History Society, Autumn 1986)

Parker, Mike, *Mapping the Roads* (AA Publishing, 2013)

Parnell, Sir Henry, *A Treatise on Roads* (1833)

Parsons, E J S, *The Map of Great Britain circa AD 1360 known as The Gough Map: an introduction to the facsimile* (Oxford, 1970)

Pawson, Eric, *Transport and Economy: The Turnpike Roads of Eighteenth Century England* (Academic Press Inc, 1977)

Pearce, Rhoda M, *Thomas Telford*, 2nd edition (Oxford: Shire Publications, 1978)

Pennant, Thomas, *The Journey from Chester to London* (read online, published Wilkie and Robinson, London, 1811)

Pepys, Samuel, *Diary of Samuel Pepys* (1893 edition, Project Gutenberg, http://www.gutenberg.org)

Philpott, Trevor, 'The Road to Disaster: A Judgment on the A5', *Picture Post*, pp.12–16 (12 February 1955)

Pratt's High Test Plan of Watling Street, and principal roads from Dover to Holyhead (undated)

Pryor, F, *The Making of the British Landscape* (London, Penguin, 2010)

Quartermaine, J, and others, *Thomas Telford's Holyhead Road* (York, Council for British Archaeology, 2003)

Rack, Henry D, *Reasonable Enthusiast: John Wesley and the Rise of Methodism* (Epworth Press, 1989)

Rocque, John, Map of the London End of the Holyhead Road (1746)

Rolt, L T C, *Thomas Telford* (Revised edition, Sutton Publishing Limited, 2007)

Roucoux, Omer, *The Roman Watling Street* (Dunstable Museum Trust, 1984)

Sawyer, Peter, *The Wealth of Anglo-Saxon England* (Oxford, Oxford University Press, 2013)

Short, Brian, *England's Landscape: The South East* (London, English Heritage/Collins, 2006)

Slack, Paul, *Poverty and Policy in Tudor and Stuart England* (London, Longman, 1988)

Stenton, Sir Frank, *Anglo-Saxon England* (Oxford, Clarendon Press,1943)

Stenton, Sir Frank, *The Roads of the Gough Map*, in Parsons E J S (ed) *Map of Great Britain c AD 1360 known as the Gough map* (Oxford, Bodleian Library, 1958)

Sunderland, John and Webb, Margaret (Eds.), *Towcester: The Story of an English Country Town* (1995)

Tacitus, *The Annals of Imperial Rome* (trans Michael Grant, Penguin, 1956, repr 1996)

Tanner, J R, *Tudor Constitutional Documents* (Cambridge, Cambridge University Press, 1951)

Taylor, C, *Roads and Tracks of Britain* (London, Dent, 1979)

Taylor, John, *Carriers Cosmographie* (1637)

Trinder, Barrie (Ed.), *Victorian Shrewsbury* (Shrewsbury, 1984)

Upton, Chris, *A History of Birmingham* (Chichester, Phillimore, 1993)

Victoria County History (several volumes consulted and referenced, available through British History Online, at www.british-history.ac.uk)

Warren, W L, *Henry II* (London, Eyre Methuen, 1973)

Webb, Diana, *Pilgrimage in Medieval England* (London, A&C Black, 2000)

Weir, Alison, *The Princes in the Tower* (The Bodley Head, 1992)

Wesley, John (ed. Parker), *The Journal of John Wesley*, 1951 (The Christian Classics Ethereal Library online)

Westminster City Council, 'Working for the Future of Edgware Road', consultation paper (2006)

White, Roger and Barker, Philip, *Wroxeter: the Life and Death of a Roman City* (Tempus Publishing, 1998)

Williams, Herbert, *Stage Coaches in Wales* (Barry, 1977)

Wilson, Kevin, 'The English Market Town' (website: www.familysearch.org/learn/wiki/en/The_English_Market_Town)

List of Illustrations and Maps

Index

About the Author

Andrew Hudson was born in the Birmingham area. For decades, his career in public services meant that his enthusiasm for writing went into government reports and strategy documents. Now free of those duties, he has combined his interests in history, exploring, and writing in this book. He lives in London.